THE Adult Learner's Guide to College Success

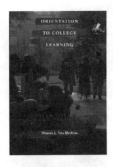

Also available from the Wadsworth College Success™ Series:

Orientation to College Learning (1995)
by Dianna L. Van Blerkom
ISBN 0-534-24528-5

I Know What It Says …What Does It Mean? Critical Skills for Critical Reading (1995)
by Daniel J. Kurland
ISBN 0-534-24486-6

Learning Your Way Through College (1995)
by Robert N. Leamnson
ISBN 0-534-24504-8

Your Transfer Planner: Strategic Tools and Guerrilla Tactics (1995)
by Carey E. Harbin
ISBN 0-534-24372-X

Toolkit for College Success (1994)
by Daniel R. Walther
ISBN 0-534-23052-0

Pocket Toolkit (interactive software, 1994)
by Daniel R. Walther and Glaser Media Group
ISBN 0-534-23068-7 (Macintosh), 0-534-23056-3 (IBM)

Mastering Mathematics: How to Be a Great Math Student, Second Edition (1994)
by Richard Manning Smith
ISBN 0-534-20838-X

Turning Point (1993)
by Joyce D. Weinsheimer
ISBN 0-534-19422-2

Merlin: The Sorcerer's Guide to Survival in College (1990)
by Christopher F. Monte
ISBN 0-534-13482-3

Also available from the Freshman Year Experience™ Series:

The Power to Learn: Helping Yourself to College Success
by William E. Campbell (1993)
ISBN 0-534-19404-4

To get your copies of the above Wadsworth titles, please visit your local bookseller.

THE *Adult Learner's Guide to College Success*

REVISED EDITION

Laurence N. Smith
Eastern Michigan University

Timothy L. Walter
University of Illinois, Chicago

Wadsworth Publishing Company

I⊤P™ **An International Thomson Publishing Company**

Belmont • Albany • Bonn • Boston • Cincinnati • Detroit • London • Madrid • Melbourne
Mexico City • New York • Paris • San Francisco • Singapore • Tokyo • Toronto • Washington

College Success Editor: Angela Gantner Wrahtz
Assistant Editor: Lisa Timbrell
Editorial Assistant: Kate Peltier
Production Editor: Michelle Filippini
Text Designer: Irene Imfeld
Print Buyer: Diana Spence
Permissions Editor: Robert Kauser
Copy Editor: Jennifer Gordon
Cover Designer: Nicole Arigoni
Compositor: Fog Press
Printer: Malloy Lithographing, Inc.

COPYRIGHT © 1995 by Wadsworth Publishing Company
A Division of International Thomson Publishing Inc.

I(T)P The ITP logo is a trademark under license.
Printed in the United States of America
  2 3 4 5 6 7 8 9 10—01 00 99 98 97 96

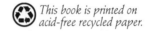 *This book is printed on
acid-free recycled paper.*

For more information, contact Wadsworth Publishing Company.

Wadsworth Publishing Company
10 Davis Drive
Belmont, California 94002, USA

International Thomson Editores
Campos Eliseos 385, Piso 7
Col. Polanco
11560 México D.F. México

International Thomson Publishing Europe
Berkshire House 168-173
High Holborn
London, WC1V 7AA, England

International Thomson Publishing GmbH
Königswinterer Strasse 418
53227 Bonn, Germany

Thomas Nelson Australia
102 Dodds Street
South Melbourne 3205
Victoria, Australia

International Thomson Publishing Asia
221 Henderson Road
#05-10 Henderson Building
Singapore 0315

Nelson Canada
1120 Birchmount Road
Scarborough, Ontario
Canada M1K 5G4

International Thomson Publishing Japan
Hirakawacho Kyowa Building, 3F
2-2-1 Hirakawacho
Chiyoda-ku, Tokyo 102, Japan

Library of Congress Cataloging-in-Publication Data
Smith, Laurence N.
   Adult learner's guide to college success / Laurence N.
Smith, Timothy L. Walter. — Rev. ed.
      p.   cm.
   Rev. ed. of: The mountain is high unless you take the
elevator. © 1992.
Includes bibliographical references.
   ISBN: 0-534-23298-1 (acid-free paper)
   1. Study skills.   2. Adult education—United States.
3. Students—United States—Time management.   4. Learn-
ing.   I. Walter, Tim.   II. Smith, Laurence N.   Mountain is
high unless you take the elevator.   III. Title.
LC5225.M47S65   1995
374'.1302812—dc20   94-34194

To five outstanding teachers:

Glenn Knudsvig
Ronald O. Lippitt
James V. McConnell
Richard A. Siggelkow
Donald E. P. Smith

Contents

Preface

This book is written specifically for adult learners who are working full- or part-time, managing families, changing careers and, for a hundred different reasons, are going back to college. We have focused on the issues identified by adults as the most critical to their academic success. You will find these issues presented in three sections: Managing Yourself; Surviving in the Learning Environment; and Learning How to Learn. To be successful, adult learners have told us that they must know *what to change* in their approach to college and *how to change* themselves. The strategies in this book are geared to help you make these changes and achieve your goals. By taking advantage of the discoveries and strategies in the book, you will attain your educational goals in less time and with less stress.

Key Features: Each chapter has key features that help you accomplish your goals and that make the book easy and useful. Although chapters within the section are connected thematically, each chapter may be used independently. The chapters are designed so that you can assess your strengths and the ways in which you want to improve quickly. This book will help you:

- Increase your strengths and improve your efficiency and effectiveness with new learning strategies.

- Meet the challenges you face combining career and family responsibilities with new educational experiences.

- Recognize the advantages you have as an adult learner in competing with younger students.

- Improve your time-management skills and other skills that need strengthening.

- Plan your major and select your courses the SMART way.

- Choose the right career and get the job you want upon graduation.

- Gain support for your efforts as an adult learner from people who are important to you.

The strategies for your success are clearly described in each chapter. You should read and respond to all of the strategies. There are many ideas, suggestions, and approaches that, if pursued, would contribute not only to your success but also to your ease in achieving it. Once you have decided which strategies are best for you, you can use the action steps and exercises in each chapter to assist you immediately in applying the strategies to your work and to your life.

Chapter 1 introduces you to the book. It explores your perception of yourself as an adult learner. It will help you see that the key to your success is not how you will be taught but how you decide to learn. You will be able to assess how comfortable you are as an adult learner as well as where and how you might want to change your current practices and strategies for success.

Chapters 2 and 3 in Section One will help you understand how to organize and manage your life to achieve your academic, professional, and personal goals. Additionally, you will learn how managing yourself is the key to managing your time. When you complete these chapters you will have developed both a Personal Action Plan as well as a Time-Management Plan. Both of these chapters provide detailed planning forms and charts with examples—as well as supplemental material in the Appendices. These materials have been used extensively by other adult learners with excellent results. The contents and examples in these chapters will strongly contribute to your success—not only in school but also at home and at work. Chapter 4 will prepare you to get the most out of your academic advising experience, help you to choose your courses the SMART way, and lead you to develop a graduation plan. Chapter 5 will provide you with tools for selecting the right career and obtaining the job you want upon graduation. For those of you already satisfied with your career path and your job, this chapter will serve as a valuable evaluation and developmental resource.

Section Two, Surviving in the Learning Environment, begins with Chapter 6, Three Strategies for Succeeding in the Classroom, which will help you assess your academic and personal strengths. Knowledge of these strengths will give you the best position from which to make the classroom and campus experience more pleasant and productive. There are real advantages to being an adult learner, and this chapter will help you to recognize them. We know from our own experience, as well as from the experiences of successful adult learners, that one of the most important influences in attaining academic goals is having the ongoing support from an instructor coupled with the support of a group of fellow students. So, Chapter 7 is an excellent starting point for pursuing these goals. Chapter 8 will help you develop strategies to get family, friends, co-workers, and others to support your goals and objectives. You will learn how to help people close to you understand the value, to them, of your success. For many adult learners, gaining support from the people who affect their lives is at the top of the priority list. You want people supporting your efforts rather than creating frustrations and roadblocks.

Section Three, Learning How to Learn, provides the core strategies for classroom success. Chapters 9–12 in this section focus on the skills of efficient and effective learning: reading, listening, note taking, critical thinking, test preparation, and test taking. We have presented these strategies in ways you will find refreshing. We want you to see immediately how these strategies may be applied inside and outside of the classroom. The chapters and success strategies in Section Three, as is true throughout the book, can be used in any sequence. The book has been written to enable adult learners to work independently or in small groups.

The numerous exercises, self-assessments, and practical examples provided in the book will give instructors an opportunity to create stimulating classroom environments, and they will provide adult learners with the opportunities to gain the confidence necessary for their academic pursuits and to develop the appropriate patterns for success. Instructors will find the book of great value in helping adult learners face the challenges inherent in the transition to new learning environments. To make the book lively our approach is conversational, using symbols, examples, and words from everyday life.

We want to share the above perspectives to enhance your use of the book, whether you are an adult learner or an instructor. As a part of classroom situations or self-help programs, we trust that you will find the book easy to use. We welcome your reactions and comments. We have spent many years listening to adult learners and their instructors. This book is shaped by their insights. We hope to keep learning from all of you.

Tim Walter would like to note his appreciation for the continuing support of his colleague Glenn Knudsvig. He also wishes to thank his wife, Beverly, and their children, Jeremy, Kate, and Sarah, for their inspiration and encouragement.

Larry Smith wishes to thank his colleagues for contributing so many ideas over the years and, especially, for their willingness to provide the opportunities to test the numerous strategies that are the foundation for this book. He also wishes to thank his wife, Joanne, and their children, David, Emily, and Julie, for their understanding and support and their willingness to try out so many new ideas.

Both authors wish to thank Deborah DeZure, for her reviews of the first edition; Ross Oliver, for his assistance with the time-management section; and Teri Papp, for her tremendous support in preparing the manuscript and for handling the numerous details associated with this effort. We also want to express our appreciation to Kevin Hurlahe, Assistant Director of Academic Advising at Eastern Michigan University, for contributing Chapter 4, Six Strategies for Planning Your Major and Selecting Your Courses. We also thank Karen Simpkins, Associate Director of Career Services at Eastern Michigan University, for contributing Chapter 5, Three Strategies for Selecting the Right Career and Getting the Job You Want. We know these chapters enrich this revised edition and provide valuable insight and direction for adult learners. Finally, Anthony Fisher's illustrations help to enliven this edition and enhance the text.

The publisher sent a draft of the manuscript to the following instructors, who provided much helpful criticism: Mary Mandeville, Oklahoma State University; Cathie Hatch, Bemidji State; Greg Smith, University of Wisconsin Center–Rock County; Laurance J. Riley, Milwaukee Area Technical College; Gary Pierson, Pittsburg State University; Beverly Wesley, Moorhead State University; Edna F. Wilson, La Salle University; Victoria Trotter, Houston Community College; and Wanda Manning, Roane State Community College.

We would also like to thank the instructors who reviewed the revised edition of *The Adult Learner's Guide to College Success:* Fran Butler, University of Arkansas; M. L. Petty, Mississippi University for Women; Terri Samuelson, Waubonsee Community College; Jacquelyn Scott, Morehead State University; and Monroe Simpson, Conners State College.

Finally, we wish to express our deepest appreciation to our Wadsworth friends: Henry Staat, who started us on this project, and Angie Gantner Wrahtz, Lisa Timbrell, and Kate Peltier who, along with other members of their very able team, have been uniformly generous with their expertise.

CHAPTER 1

Introduction

America has become a learning society. We no longer leave school behind forever when we start work. It is likely that all of us will be going back and forth between school and work for all of our productive years. Adult learners constitute more than 43 percent of the nation's 13.1 million college students. In addition to the nearly 5.7 million adult college students, more than 35.5 million adults are engaged in formal employer-sponsored learning. Hundreds of thousands of adults are also learning through televised instruction, in the military, and in the courses, seminars, and workshops of their professional associations, community centers, and social and religious groups. Adults account for more than $100 billion of educational expenditures every year just in formal educational settings.

All of this is to say that adult learners are an important, large, and growing segment of our society. As an adult learner, you are not alone and your situation is not as unusual as you may think. Nonetheless, you may well have concerns about your entry or reentry into higher education and your ability to achieve your goals.

This book has been written expressly for adult learners. It has been developed to respond to the concerns and needs characteristic of adult learners such as yourself. It reflects our beliefs that adult learners can and will succeed and that there are strategies, tactics, and tools that can assist them as they pursue their academic, professional, and personal goals. These strategies for success are based on extensive research we have conducted with thousands of adult learners, instructors, and program administrators, focusing on strategies that encourage adults to aim for and attain their learning goals.

Who Are Adult Learners and What Do We Know About Them?

Researchers on adult learners agree that, in general, adults seek to learn in order to cope with change in their lives. Almost all adult learners point to their own changing circumstances as their reason for learning. They are, in short, a group of individuals who are in transition, moving from one status or situation to another. Adults in transition want to learn what they need to know in order to be successful in their new roles. Although many adults enjoy learning for its own sake, most learn because they want to acquire new knowledge and skills.

The overwhelming majority of adult students work, and most work full-time, outside or inside the home. Most of them are women, but there is a substantial population of adult men in college as well. A large majority of adult learners are married or have been married and have family responsibilities. These adults are extraordinarily busy people—juggling work, family, and studies.

But if, in fact, most adults seek to learn in order to cope with change in their lives, then strategies for success must include strategies for change. In many respects, this entire book is about change. It focuses on strategies, tactics, and tools you can use for your academic success, but these approaches can be used to change personal and professional areas of your life as well.

These strategies are organized into three strands, each of them crucial to your success: time management and self-management, self-change, and learning skills. We believe that these three strands provide you with a helpful framework for exploring your personal situation and achieving success.

Our approach in this book requires your active involvement. During your exploration of each of the three strands, you will find opportunities to build upon your experiences, needs, and goals. You will be asked to participate while you read and to complete exercises and activities. You can use the information you generate about yourself to determine the best approaches for you as an individual.

We have divided the book into three sections:

- Section One: Managing Yourself

- Section Two: Surviving in the Learning Environment

- Section Three: Learning How to Learn

These sections may be used together or independently. Thus you can start wherever you wish and develop the strategies and action steps that reflect your particular situation and that will have immediate payoffs for your success. As your needs change, you may find other sections of greater assistance.

The Key to Success Is Not How You Are Taught but How You Learn

To begin, we urge you to look first at yourself as a learner, because the key to your success is not how you are taught but how you learn. In the past, higher education was primarily instructor-focused; now it is increasingly learner-focused. In an instructor-focused environment, the instructor determines what you learn, when you learn, and how you learn. In a learner-focused environment, it is up to you, the learner, to make these decisions. In the face of conflicting learning goals or a lack of direction or relevance in the learning situation, it may be up to you to restructure the instructor-focused environment and translate it into a learner-focused one for your own personal success. But to do that effectively, you need to understand your needs and skills as a learner.

How you approach learning as an adult will be determined initially by how you approached learning in your last formal learning situation—whether it was high school, college, or any of the many other situations we noted above. The more education you have, the more likely you are to engage in additional learning. We also know that there are strong pressures for you to learn because of changing requirements in the way you do your work and in the workplace itself. Others of you are responding to demands in your personal lives. These pressures exist whether you are working in a factory, a hospital, at home, or in a corporate office, and whether you are self-employed or among the ranks of hourly or managerial employees.

You have to learn how to learn because the rapid pace at which new information is created requires you to become your own curriculum development specialist as well as your own teacher. By the year 2000, according to *The Futurist* magazine (November/December 1988), the amount of knowledge available will have multiplied four times. In that single year alone you will be exposed to more information and knowledge than your grandparents experienced in their lifetimes.

Assessing Your Comfort Level for Learning and Change

Several personal factors influence your readiness to learn and your willingness to change. First, there are your attitudes toward learning and your comfort level with it as a result of earlier learning experiences. Second, there are forces in your current work and personal life that determine whether you take advantage of learning opportunities. And finally, there are your ability and willingness to tolerate moderate levels of discomfort as you learn to survive and succeed in new learning situations.

Many adults have shared their feelings about their readiness for learning and for change. Their thoughts are listed below. Check (✔) the ones that express how you feel (or might feel) about your new learning experience, and add to the list any others that describe your situation.

- ❏ I'm too old.
- ❏ I don't like studying even though my job requires me constantly to learn new information and skills.
- ❏ I didn't do well the first time; I'm not certain how I'll do now.
- ❏ I'm excited about learning. It's not only stimulating but you meet a lot of interesting people.
- ❏ I can't believe how welcome I've been made to feel. It's obvious the instructors and administrators have had a lot of experience with adult learners; they're very responsive.
- ❏ They're really responsive to adult learners—they even have an orientation program on videotape.
- ❏ There are special offices to serve adult learners and they're open when I'm here.
- ❏ They form study and support groups and give us time to meet during class.
- ❏ Things are always coming up to keep me from finishing what I've started. I can't help it that there are so many demands on my time.
- ❏ Instructors are always very friendly and helpful. They want you to succeed.
- ❏ There are many people and programs that can help you to be successful.
- ❏ I'm too busy to take advantage of the special help I need.

❑ Asking for help is a sign of weakness. It's best for me to work this out on my own.

❑ Wouldn't it be great if someone would pass around the names and telephone numbers of others in this learning situation? If I had trouble, then I could call them.

❑ I would never call a classmate for help. It wouldn't be something I'd be comfortable doing.

❑ This is the greatest opportunity for securing the future I've ever had.

❑ I know I'll be successful because I've always been successful.

❑ I know I'll be successful because I enjoy learning.

❑ I'm concerned that if I don't do well, my employer will think I'm not competent.

❑ I've always had butterflies when I've started something new or different.

❑ I would learn best if I could learn with a friend.

❑ This isn't the first time I've started a learning experience, but it will be the first time I've finished one.

❑ I wouldn't be in this situation if I weren't being forced into it by my employer.

❑ There are so many other adult learners that I feel very much at ease.

❑ I never did well on tests and I'm uncomfortable now.

❑ To tell you the truth, even though I'm very successful at work, I'm nervous about this.

❑ I haven't taken a test in so long I'm concerned about how well I'll do.

❑ I think I'm too old to be learning.

❑ All of the brochures and materials about this program seem to be focused on much younger learners.

❑ I like learning, but I'm very rusty.

❑ I'm a very successful person. I feel very much in control at work and at school. I'll do well because I always do well.

Things that I'm thinking and feeling that aren't listed above:

❑ ....

❑ ....

❑ ....

❑ ....

❑ ....

The statements above—statements that have been made by numerous adult learners—reflect a wide range of attitudes and experiences. The reason we asked you to check the ones that best describe how you feel (or might feel) is to remind you that you are not alone in your thoughts and feelings.

Whether you are in business or in construction, a homemaker returning to school after raising your children or a factory worker taking an on-site course, being placed in a new learning environment may rekindle feelings and attitudes that take you back to earlier times in your life when you were a student. You probably had different needs, skills, and values then, and the influences exerted by your family and peer group were different. All the same, the way you feel about learning today has been shaped by your earlier experiences. Even though you've changed a lot since then, memories of past learning experiences may awaken old anxieties and fears.

If you have checked statements that reflect concern about your personal comfort or the responsiveness of your new learning environment, don't worry—you are among the vast majority of adult learners.

Research on adult learners indicates that the most successful people have been those who, despite their fears or uncertainties, asked for help when they felt they needed it. We hope you will approach your learning environment assertively, overcoming the voices of doubt within you, and that you will take advantage of the services and people available to you. They are there to help you help yourself.

SECTION ONE

Managing Yourself

CHAPTER 2

Action Planning for Personal Success

This book is about change, because learning effectively and achieving your goals will involve change for you, probably in many areas of your life. A return to school affects the people who are important in your life, your daily routines, and your priorities. And we know that making changes in an established life pattern to accommodate an academic schedule can be as challenging as any of the coursework you will encounter as a student. For this reason, we have felt it important to focus first on how to shape and organize your life in ways that will make it possible for you to change and to achieve your goals, whether they are academic, professional, or personal.

You have learned in Chapter 1 that *your academic success depends* not on how well you are taught but *on how well you learn*. In other words, you personally have to assume full responsibility for your own educational success. This is a central concept of the change process we think works best, not only in your academic pursuits but in all areas of your life. This concept places the burden of attaining success on you, not on your teachers, your co-workers, your boss, your family, or your friends. Remember, the person you can change most easily is you, and you are the one who will benefit most from your success.

You might say this is obvious, but many adult learners we have talked with feel that other people control their lives. Poor teachers, mean-spirited supervisors, incompetent co-workers, insensitive spouses, and selfish children are only some of the people they think control their destinies. When we explore the situation with them, it quickly becomes obvious to them that they have fallen into the trap of blaming someone else for their problems and thus giving that person control over them.

This is not the place to explore in depth why some of us let others have control over our lives. But having raised the point, we must emphasize that your success depends on your willingness to accept responsibility for your own behavior and consequently for your own future. Thus, whether you become the beneficiary of change or its victim depends on how you individually choose to act.

Another change concept we touched upon earlier is that *how you assess your opportunity for change depends on your mind-set*. Even very adverse situations offer many opportunities for success. But the ability to see opportunities rather than insoluble problems will be determined as much by your mind-set as by the situation itself. We pointed out that how you, as an adult, approach a new learning situation may initially be determined by the mind-set you developed in the course of your experience in your earlier formal educational situations. Our current pathways to change usually are pretty well determined by our past experiences. And so they should be, for we learn how to approach the future from what we experience as we go along.

But past experiences aren't always the best guide to our success. The past can be a dangerous guide if the future includes new elements or forces that were absent from the past. And because we live in a rapidly changing world, it is important to scan our environment continuously for forces (events, developments, and trends) that are influencing what we want to accomplish. The mind-set with which we scan the environment for these forces will very often determine what we see and how we see it. Very often it is important to shift our mind-set to get an accurate reading of the opportunities that truly present themselves and assess how we can effectively or efficiently use them to achieve our dreams and goals.

Therefore, we suggest that if you want to be successful, it is necessary to *let go of the past* and to focus on the future you desire so that you can develop the necessary new pathways and approaches to it. This is the process we refer to as *creating your preferred future*.

The best way to focus on the future is to create a vision of what your preferred future will look like. Once you have created the vision of your preferred future, it becomes necessary to translate it into concrete reality by restating it clearly and concisely in terms that are oriented toward end results that are time-bounded and measurable.

While this book is designed to provide you with the tools and techniques you need to achieve exceptional academic results, we also keenly recognize that if we are to achieve our dreams and goals, most of us have to change the way we approach them. Mastering content, more often than not, isn't enough. The processes we use, our approaches to learning and to life, are even more important in bringing about the desired outcomes we want—our preferred future.

In this chapter, building upon the change strategies we've identified and others that we will explore in more detail later, we provide you with a method to develop a step-by-step action plan to help you achieve your personal success. It was developed in response to adult learners who recognized that the central challenge they faced was coping with change.

One man who returned to an academic setting after many years in the workplace expressed concerns common to many adult learners:

> *How can I change myself so that I will do well in school and get my degree? My employer has really forced me back to college. I didn't like high school and I didn't like college any better. I never could stand the slow pace of school and especially how boring studying was. Oh, I did what was necessary to get by, but I jumped at the first chance I had to reach my goals without completing my education. I've always liked working and learning has been easier on the job and more exciting than in a classroom. There are more rewards in a job well done than in getting a passing grade, no matter how high it is. At least that's true for me. But now I have a new boss who insists that I have a college degree in order to be promoted. At least he's paying for my degree, but I have to do it while I'm still working.*
>
> *The thing that worries me is that I have to be successful in school now to be successful in work. The knowledge I gain will be important, but without good grades and a degree I can't be promoted. It's strange, they hired me*

without a college degree and I've done well, but now there's no future for me without one. I wish I had stuck it out the first time through, before I got married and had a family. Now I've got a job, a family, and a new boss that insists I go back and get my degree.

I want to stay with the company and be promoted; it represents a great opportunity and will also bring a large increase in salary. But it certainly also will be a major change in my life for the next couple of years. At one point I was thinking of looking for a new job, but you know my boss was right when he told me that without a college degree no one would even hire me, at least not at my current level and salary.

This is only one of many change scenarios we have reviewed. Here are a few lines from some others:

To be successful I need to become more assertive in order to compete better.

I need to change my self-confidence; I wish I had the guts just to quit and find a better job.

My husband is very old-fashioned and it bothers him that I'm out of the house so much while I pursue a college degree. He wants me to wait until the children are completely grown, but by then it will be too late for me. I want a life outside the home. The change I need to make is to learn how to confront my husband and my family and not allow them to create anxiety that causes me to jeopardize my educational goals.

They're hiring all these kids right out of college and they're making more than I am. I've got to train them so that they can be my boss, so I decided I ought to go to college. Well, here I am. What I've got to change is everything. Throughout my whole life I was proving I could make it without a college degree. Now I want to learn and I want to go to school and pass my courses and earn a degree.

My husband recently died from a sudden heart attack. There is enough financial support for a modest life and I could rely on my children if it were absolutely necessary, but I wouldn't want to, even as a last resort. I have a college degree, but it's so outdated; and since I decided it's time for me to learn a new career, I've enrolled for courses to credential myself before I go on the job market. I'm as frightened as I can be. It's strange, but after twenty-eight years of marriage I'm independent again. I guess I really need to change how I approach my new status and life itself.

Although each of these change scenarios is unique in some way, they all have in common an underlying need for change and adaptation. You too have your own unique set of circumstances that surround your decision to return to school and that will affect your efforts and your success. Use the following materials to help you identify the important parts of your own change scenario so that you can then develop your own personal action plan to help you succeed.

Your Personal Action Plan

A filled-in action plan is provided in Appendix 1. You may wish to refer to this material as you complete your personal action plan. Blank sets of forms are also included for you to use.

Action Step 1   ***Develop your change scenario:*** A change scenario is a short essay about yourself similar to the comments you have read earlier. Write about what's happening in your life that is creating an interest in or a need to change. In other words, describe your opportunities for change.

....

....

....

....

....

....

....

....

....

Action Step 2   ***Describe your vision for change—your preferred future:*** What will happen to you as a result of the change you envision? When you write, imagine that the change has already taken place and describe what you or your situation look like as though it had already happened. Write, therefore, in the present tense. Describe how things look, how they differ from the way they used to be. And don't forget to indicate what month and year this is so that you will know how long you have given yourself to implement your vision for change.

....

....

....

....

....

....

....

....

Action Step 3   ***Translate your vision into goal statements:*** List your goals in the accompanying table and indicate whether they are for the short term (one to two years), the intermediate term (three to four years), or the long term (five or more years). Then restate those goals to indicate what they will look like when you've achieved them.

Goal number	Goal statement	How it will look when achieved	Time frame (years) 1–2	3–4	5+

Action Step 4   ***List in the accompanying table all positive or facilitating forces you can think of that will help you achieve each goal you have listed:*** Forces can be *within yourself* (I want to earn more money; I want to be promoted) or *within your family* (my children are grown up and out of the house; we need extra income to pay for our children's college) or *within your work or learning environment* (I have a new boss who demands that I get a college degree; I want to be able to compete with new employees who are better educated than I am). As you develop this analysis you will find that some forces are moving you toward more than one goal. It's not necessary to list a force more than once; just note all the goals each force facilitates.

Action Step 5   ***List in the accompanying table all negative or blocking forces that will impede your progress toward each goal you have identified:*** Again, it's not necessary to repeat any force that is blocking your progress toward more than one goal; just note all the goals each force is blocking. Some blocking forces we've heard about: "I'm frightened about the change." "I didn't go to school originally because I wasn't sure I would be successful." "With all these years that have passed I've probably forgotten even how to study." "My husband and children say they need me at home full-time." "My boss expects me to go to school, but my co-workers expect me to produce just as much and participate in extra overload assignments." "Every time I have a test or paper due, my boss sends me out of town or makes me work overtime."

Action Step 4	**Action Step 5**
List all positive or facilitating forces	List all negative or blocking forces
Inside yourself	
Within your family and other relationships	
Within your work or learning environment	

Action Step 6   ***Review Action Steps 4 and 5 and mark with an asterisk(*) the facilitating and blocking forces you can do something about immediately:*** Focus on these forces first. As time goes on you can work on the others, but it's important to have a starting point. It's best to start with what can be changed *now*.

Action Step 7   ***Mobilize for change:*** Review the forces you marked with an asterisk (*) in Action Steps 4 and 5. Transfer the facilitating forces to the lefthand column of the following table. For each force you have recorded in the lefthand column, list all the ideas, means, and resources you can use to make these forces work more strongly for you.

Action Step 8   ***Mobilize for change:*** Review the forces you marked with an asterisk (*) in Action Steps 4 and 5. Transfer the blocking forces to the righthand column of the following table. For each force you have recorded in the righthand column, list all the ideas, means, and resources you can use to remove or cope with these forces.

Action Step 7	*Action Step 8*
Facilitating forces	**Blocking forces**
Force:	**Force:**
Force:	**Force:**
Force:	**Force:**

Action Step 9   ***Determine major change tactics:*** Review all of the information in Action Steps 7 and 8 and decide which ones are critical for achieving your goals. Write each of your change tactics in the accompanying table.

Action Step 10   ***Create a comprehensive action plan:*** Number the square in front of each change tactic to indicate the order in which these steps should be taken. After you have completed Action Steps 9 and 10, we suggest you rewrite your action plan in priority order, following the format of the accompanying table.

	Change tactics	Members of my change team who should be involved	Other resources available	Anticipated completion date
☐				
☐				
☐				
☐				
☐				
☐				
☐				
☐				
☐				
☐				

Action Step 11   ***Describe what early progress will look like for each change tactic:*** State each step in clear and concise terms that are oriented toward your end results.

Action Step 12   ***Keep things moving forward:*** Identify what needs to be done to keep things progressing toward your goals.

	Action Step 11	*Action Step 12*
Change tactic number	**Progress description**	**What needs to be done to move ahead**

Action Step 13   ***Review and revise your plan each week or as appropriate:*** This is a crucial step. As you proceed through school and face the challenges that lie ahead in your life, circumstances will change. There will be new goals and new forces that will help and hinder you, but you will be equipped with a powerful way to analyze the situation and to develop successful strategies to achieve your goals.

CHAPTER 3

Five Strategies for Time Management

Strategy 1: Visualize yourself as you would like to be

Strategy 2: Organize for your success

Strategy 3: Get others to help you

Strategy 4: Overcome your tendency to procrastinate

Strategy 5: Reward yourself for success

You are in a hurry. Well, so am I in a hurry. Time is very important to me. I wear a watch on my wrist. I have a clock on my desk, a clock in my car, and several in my house, and when I wake up in the middle of the night, the first thing I do is look and see what time it is. When I travel I even carry a small clock in my briefcase, but I often don't need it because my hotel room has a clock, the TV in the hotel room also has a clock built in, and I can even call the operator to learn the time or arrange for a wake-up call. Even my pocket calculator has a built-in clock.

On my way to work I drive by two buildings that have clocks on their signs. The announcer on my favorite radio station reminds me of the time between the songs and the commercials. There's a channel on my TV that runs the time along the bottom of the screen. And I should point out that on my desk telephone at work one of the programmed telephone numbers is the one that announces the time.

When I'm at home my wife and kids are always asking me the time, so I'm always looking at my watch and I'm very conscious of it. And when I'm at work my secretary's always reminding me what time it is and how late I'll be if I don't leave now.

Almost every day the mail brings at least one brochure, and usually several, telling me about time-management systems, special calendars that have been turned into bulky notebooks with lots of sections. I'm invited to enroll in time-management seminars and workshops, buy tapes and books, and subscribe to newsletters either for myself or for my staff. There are even time-management consultants who will personally visit with me or my staff to help us understand how busy we are so that we will interrupt each other only for something really urgent or at times that we have specially set aside for interruptions.

And if all this isn't enough, I keep coming across articles about time-management techniques in magazines, newspapers, and journals. Everyone I run into tells me how busy they are, how fast they're running to keep in place, how little time they have, how late they go to bed, how early they get up, how much time everything they do ends up taking, and how each day ends with another chorus of "There just aren't enough hours in the day."

And apparently there really aren't enough hours in the day. As a result, all kinds of new services are being provided, from house cleaning to personal shopping. Someone will deliver to you practically anything you can buy that you'd ever want. There are also shopping and valet services galore. If fast food isn't fast enough, I can buy food already prepared at the supermarket. In my neighborhood you can also call in an order at several restaurants, and a delivery service will drive around to pick up your meal and deliver it to your door.

There is no question that matters related to time are near the top of Americans' agenda. The question is: How can we (or do we) pay for the time we save? Most of us pay for it emotionally and financially by working harder to make more money (or at least to justify the expense in our own minds) so that we may afford these time-saving services.

Whatever our situation, these are just some of the pressures and thoughts that have driven us into an obsession over time management. Ironically, every one of us has all the time there is, but it seems that no matter how busy or productive we are, we still don't have enough time to accomplish what we want to do.

The issues come quickly into focus. How can we do more in the time we have? How can we eliminate or reduce the pressures of not having enough time to get everything done (with or without quality) and still have personal time, whether for relaxing, sports, or socializing with our friends or family, and the most important thing, for not feeling guilty about enjoying ourselves even if we could be doing something else more "productive"?

The Key to Time Management Is Really Self-Management

Time management is really only a tool of self-management. Time management will not make self-management work, but, self-management is what makes time management work effectively.

Time management is the art of balancing your efforts, putting things in focus; it requires attention to what's important to do to achieve your goals and to control or cope with those intrusions that deter or detract you from what you need to do.

Time management requires you to make choices and postpone short-term gratifications for long-term gains. Managing your time means overcoming the bad habits that allow you to put off what needs to be done. It means controlling yourself and your energy to produce a good effect on your work, home, and school environments. It requires you to set goals and make plans for attaining them. When you learn to manage your time you acquire organizational skills, and because you have determined how long things really take and when you can do them, anxiety and stress ought to recede. Time management also frees up your mind, because when you do have time to relax, to enjoy yourself, you know that you honestly earned your relaxation and that you're doing what you enjoy for its intrinsic value and not as a means to put off a chore in the hope that somehow it will disappear.

We have identified five strategies that lead to extraordinary success. These strategies are interrelated and intertwined. The pursuit of each strategy helps in the mastery of the others and provides momentum for achieving your goals both effectively and efficiently.

Strategy 1   *Visualize Yourself as You Would Like to Be*

Tactic 1

Create your vision for focused action: Don't visualize yourself as you are today. Let your mind wander for a minute or two. If your hopes and wishes come to pass, how do you see yourself? Walking across the stage at commencement and receiving your diploma? Or taking a new job with a new office? Or just making more money?

Take a few minutes to draw a picture of yourself, or have someone take a photograph of you, or write out your vision of what your success will look like. If your goal is a college degree, for example, draw a cap and gown. Or better yet, borrow a cap and gown and have someone take a photograph of you in it. Post it where you will see it frequently.

Tactic 2

Translate your vision into goals and objectives: Translate that vision into a statement that spells out the end results you expect to achieve, the time frame in which you expect to achieve them, and the means by which your results can be measured. The goal of achieving a degree might be stated something like this: "By 1998 I will have finished my work for my degree. I will do so by taking two courses each fall and winter term over the next four years, and in 1997–1998 I will go full-time to finish my remaining coursework. I will receive my diploma June 1998."

This is a good goal statement because it has been translated into objectives (desired end results that are time-bounded and measurable).

Tactic 3

Develop focused action: Having focus is important. It allows you to define what will help you realize your vision and achieve your goals and objectives. Focus, in this context, is the action that takes place at the point where the outcomes of determination, persistence, and endurance converge and a clear image of what must be done emerges. Focused action is critical for planned success. It is the action that keeps you on track, moving in the right direction at the appropriate time and in the correct way. It is the bridge that links your vision—your goals and objectives—and the organization you need to develop if you are to achieve them.

An artist was asked how he was able to sculpt such a beautiful statue out of a plain block of marble. He replied that it was easy. He focused on the vision of the statue he wanted and just chipped away everything that didn't belong there. He found a way to unite his vision of his goal (the statue he wanted to create) with his plan to achieve it (to chip away everything that didn't belong in it) and focused his action (sculpting). In other words, he had *organized for success!*

Strategy 2   *Organize for Your Success*

Tactic 4

Plan on paper: If it's not written on paper (or in a computer), it's not a plan; it's only an idea. Experts agree: If it's not written out, it just doesn't get properly developed and executed.

Tactic 5   ***Create an organization center:*** Those of you fortunate enough to have a room at home or a workplace office to use as a study/command center have got it made—if it's organized to be efficient. If you don't have an extra room, the organization command center can be a kitchen cabinet, a corner of the bedroom, a closet, or even a filing box. No matter where it is or how big it is, a place to keep together the papers and plans that pertain to your home, your finances, your schoolwork, and your other activities will help you be more efficient and productive. Being organized is a time-management technique that is an important timesaver.

Tactic 6   ***Plan for the unplanned:*** The school calls and your child needs to be picked up because she isn't feeling well; your boss needs a report and you can either do the report or do your homework; illness in your family forces you to be out of town for several days during the time when you had planned to work on your term paper; your car needs work and has to be left at the garage, and you have to depend on someone who is late to drive you to school or work.

These are only a few of the hundreds of possible unplanned events that confront you when you least have the time or flexibility to attend to them. But attend to them you must! The best schedule obviously cannot accommodate large-scale interruptions without considerable difficulty. Small nuisances are barely tolerable.

Often you'll hear, "My life can't be planned. I'm so busy putting out fires, I can't get any work done." It's our strong belief that you *can* plan for the unplanned. You need to schedule your work so that you're not always doing it at the last minute or within such a tight time frame that life crashes around you at the slightest bump.

If you build some flexibility into your schedule, you will find that unplanned events can be accommodated and the stress and strain of major interruptions and emergencies will not be compounded by a schedule so tight that when one thing goes awry, everything goes haywire. Just knowing when you plan to do things—having a plan—is the best way to confront the unplanned event, because you know just what has to give and when you can get back to it. A plan with built-in flexibility is a super plus because it also provides you with an opportunity to respond to the stress of the situation without compounding it with stress over what has to be done.

Tactic 7   ***Plan to plan:*** Make sure that as you develop your schedule, you set aside time each day to reflect on what you have accomplished, your vision, your long- and short-term goals, and your progress in your efforts to achieve them. Review and update. Schedule or reschedule your next day to meet the objectives that have been set for you and that you have set for yourself. Allow some time in the planning process to daydream a little about your future and how important what you are doing is to achieving it. Often this is an excellent reward for a day's hard work and for the completion of goals and objectives on schedule.

Tactic 8   ***Plan to change:*** Every new skill takes time to learn and every new habit requires practice and time to adjust old behavior patterns. You need to recognize your limits and perhaps to stretch them. But no matter how much you can do or want to do, there are absolute limits and you must set your plans within them. This takes practice and is hard work. The payoffs are a bit down the pathway from your current efforts, and getting in shape may be tougher than you imagined.

Keeping your vision in mind makes it easier, but change, diligence, and persistence are tough taskmasters and exact a price of discomfort. Sometimes you will slip or revert to past practices. But you can build on your past gains and start out again farther along the pathway to success.

In exercise, sports, studying, or anything else you do, it's easier to keep in shape than to get into shape. When you know what skills you need to master to be successful, practicing them soon replaces counterproductive and inefficient planning efforts. You will get used to your new ways of behavior. You will find enjoyment in your new productivity—in both how you act and what you achieve.

Two big obstacles can make this task very difficult: the demands of others upon you and your own innate desire to procrastinate. Therefore, the following tactics are critical to master if these first two strategies are to be successfully pursued and consolidated into your daily routine.

Tactic 9

Develop a step-by-step action plan: Organizing for success requires the strong foundation provided by Strategy 1—*having vision for focused action*.

Many people think that making a "to do" list, having a schedule in their minds, or even keeping an appointment calendar or planning notebook is the key to planning. These activities may be important in the planning process, but they are not the same as organizing for success.

Simply put, the key to organizing for success requires a plan that you will follow to ensure that you achieve your vision—your goals and objectives. Your *plan* will be a set of coordinated actions. These actions will be linked together to achieve your predetermined results.

Your best plans will be those that are developed into a series of discrete action steps. Each step will move your effort or project toward the desired end results.

Many of your action steps will take place simultaneously, and others only sequentially. Although the boundaries between your action steps will not always be as clear as you would like them to be, there will be discrete outcomes that mark achievement. These outcomes are important to determine. They help define the steps that need to be taken and let you know whether you are on track.

In your planning you will have identified a large goal. Let's stick with the example of earning a college degree. In Tactic 2 we identified a plan to earn a degree by attending school part-time now and full-time in the final year. The overall plan includes not only a course plan but also a plan to secure a leave of absence from your job for the last year, and a financial plan to determine how you will pay your school and personal expenses. These planning outcomes serve as markers that will help determine each planning initiative and the action steps that need to be taken for its implementation and achievement. Time frames will also need to be set.

Action step-by-step planning can also be used to achieve smaller goals.

You have been assigned a 40-page history term paper, due by midterm. Your vision is to earn an A. Your goal is to write this 40-page paper within these stated requirements. Here are the action steps you might want to take:

1. *Review assignment in syllabus and talk with professor to determine dimensions of assignment and learn criteria for grade of A.*

2. *Choose a topic.*

3. *Read background material.*

4. *Develop an outline.*

5. *Conduct research.*

6. *Assemble notes and integrate them into outline.*

7. *Write and edit draft 1.*

8. *Write and edit draft 2.*

9. *Produce final copy.*

10. *Submit paper to professor.*

These 10 steps are an outline of your action plan and should be assigned a deadline to ensure that the paper is submitted by the due date.

Action step-by-step planning is an important activity—more important to success than any other, because it defines all the tasks to be done and the time frame within which they must be accomplished. Strategy 1 provides the foundation for time management; Strategy 2 provides the structure. You will also find that by following these strategies you will have the personal discipline and power to implement successfully the remaining three strategies for managing your time and yourself.

Tactic 10   ***Plan for the month, the week, and the day:*** Plan your time month by month, week by week, and day by day. Pick a time to do your planning so that it becomes a habit. During the first few days of each term, plan for that term with a month-by-month calendar. Your term (month-by-month) calendar has to be continually updated as situations change. To avoid blue Mondays and slow starts, plan for each week on the preceding Sunday afternoon, and for each day on the evening before.

Planning in this way will make you very efficient. You really will save a lot of time if you know what you have to do, when it needs to be done, and when you will do it. A filled-in set of planning forms is provided in Appendix 2. You may wish to refer to this material as you complete your own planning forms. Blank sets of forms are also included for you to use.

These forms are the heart of the many organizers available at most business supply and stationery stores and through the mail. You may wish to buy a time-management organizer or make your own in a notebook using the forms in the Appendix. Add the other sections you require, including your course syllabi, frequently used telephone numbers, notes, and other helpful information. The key is to use these sections together so they form a comprehensive approach to your work. If everything is kept together in a notebook or in backup folders, you will always know where to file away information and, even more important, where to retrieve it. That in itself is an excellent timesaver.

Strategy 3   *Get Others to Help You*

Tactic 11

Share your vision of your goals and objectives with others: If no one knows what you're attempting to do, they have no way to help you achieve your goals. Even if people can't actively help you achieve your goals, they can keep you from being successful without intending to.

People support what they help to create or build. Involving others in your efforts will motivate them to want you to succeed, especially if they know how to help. Of course, some people may be jealous or resentful of your efforts. Perhaps your spouse or your children resent your inability to spend as much time with them now and dislike having to do for themselves things that you used to do for them. Perhaps a fellow employee will see you getting ahead while he or she is not. Even your boss may fear that your success will eventually come at his or her expense.

For the most part, though, people will want to help you succeed. If they know your vision, your goals, and objectives, and your plans, they will join you on your journey. If you do not ask for their help, especially if your plans affect them, they may well feel resentment.

If resentment turns to hostility, you may need more help than any book can give you.

The main strength to be derived from sharing your objectives with others is the help they can give you if they know what your intentions are, which will then give them a sense of shared ownership and pride in your successes.

Tactic 12

Developing flexible standards: There is a significant difference between having flexible standards and lowering your standards. Many tasks creep into your daily routine because you have the time to do them or because you enjoy doing them. They may not be productive, however, and instead of helping you to move along the path toward your goals, they may serve as obstacles to your achievement. So you must be ever vigilant against becoming trapped by them.

You may clean your house less often or less thoroughly. You may wash the car less frequently. You may set aside a hobby or project. You may send your brother a check for his birthday rather than shop for a special present. You may call friends instead of writing letters to them. You may avoid calls after 9:00 P.M. to give you uninterrupted study time. You may read fewer novels or let magazines pile up unread on the coffee table. You may not go out Saturday night or you may give up a myriad of other activities that you've allowed to become rituals in your life.

At work you may volunteer for fewer committee assignments, write fewer memos about things that don't interest you, and not be available to all drop-in visitors. You may eat lunch at your desk so you can finish work that you used to take home in a briefcase at day's end but that now competes with the homework you have to do at night.

It's been said that 20 percent of your effort achieves 80 percent of your objectives. Conversely, 80 percent of your effort achieves only 20 percent of your objectives. It is important to learn which activities are most likely to lead to your goals. In time you will achieve greater efficiency and effectiveness as you direct your efforts. If you are flexible and focus on the activities that lead to your objectives, you will be rewarded for what you have left undone as well as for what you have done.

Tactic 13   ***Learn to delegate:*** "If I don't do it, it won't get done." Is that really true? It's amazing, but if it needs to be done, it will get done—and by someone else.

Children will learn to make their own lunches. Co-workers will start picking up special projects that have gravitated to your "to do" list. The supermarket and fast-food chain will be glad to do your cooking, and if you can afford it, others will be glad to clean your home, change the oil in your car, and mow your lawn.

The major thrust of this tactic, which builds on Tactics 11 and 12, is that much of what needs to be done can be delegated to others. It will be much easier for you to delegate tasks to others if they know your goals and objectives and if you're flexible in your requirements. Flexibility on your part will also make it much easier for others to accept your need for help. You may be disappointed at first, until others learn how to respond to you. You may want to jump back in to make sure the task is done correctly, but block that urge. You will see that things get done without you and that others grow as they assume greater responsibility and feel good about being able to help.

Tactic 14   ***Say no!*** The world will still function if you're not involved. People will still love and respect you if you won't get on their agenda and you will find fulfillment in achieving your goals and objectives without the distraction of tasks you let yourself get trapped into performing. It may seem easier to say yes at the time, but later on you will hate those tasks because there are other things you need and want to spend your time on.

The best way to learn to say no is to examine what you will gain personally or professionally by saying yes. If you can't just say no initially, at least say, "Let me think this over for a few days." Or say, "I'll help you today if you'll help me tomorrow." (Getting someone to watch your children, clean your house, rake your leaves, take over some outside activity, represent you on a committee, or write a memorandum for you may be a worthwhile trade-off for saying yes when you really want to say no but can't.)

Many people feel that saying no will reduce future opportunities, undermine their standing in other people's eyes, or challenge their view of their own importance. You need to say no in the context of your long-range goals and short-term objectives and in the framework of your 20/80 percent activities. Your self-esteem will get a boost if you can focus on what you started out to do and move steadily toward your goal. Saying yes may bring a good feeling to start with, but the feeling will be temporary and will soon turn into frustration, irritation, and resentment as it blocks your achievement.

Strategy 4   ***Overcome Your Tendency to Procrastinate***

Overcoming a tendency to procrastinate may be the most difficult task you face because most people have developed procrastination into an art form. What you have taken a lifetime to perfect now needs to be unlearned and replaced by a new set of behaviors.

Procrastinating, putting off what needs to be done, may be something you do consciously or unconsciously. It may reflect fear of failure or fear of success. It may be a result of a quest for perfection and a recognition that if you don't do it, it can't be evaluated, or if you do it hurriedly at the last minute, it won't be an accurate reflection of your true potential. It could be a chance to gain control over others. It could even be the result of work or emotional overload. It may come from unclear or conflicting objectives or simply be a strategy to avoid doing what you don't want to do.

You can recognize your procrastination by your behaviors. Others, however, will recognize your procrastination by its consequences.

Sometimes procrastination takes the form of socializing—writing or calling friends just to use up time. Some procrastinators sleep more, eat more, or take to daydreaming. Some take long breaks away from tasks. And others procrastinate by getting organized, by cleaning desk drawers and kitchen drawers, making "to do" lists that become substitutes for doing. Any number of procrastination behaviors are socially acceptable and look like needed release from an already busy schedule. But the consequences deserve attention.

The possible consequences include guilt and stress, anger and shortened temper, decreased motivation, and inferior results. Deadlines may constantly need to be extended and relationships may be damaged because of unmet expectations by others who count on timely, quality results. Productivity and quality diminish and personal and organizational frustration mount.

It's true, though, that a silver lining may lurk behind the cloud of procrastination. The kitchen junk drawer or office desk drawer may get organized; the house, the garage, or the basement may be cleaned; a few good magazine articles may be read. With good time management, however, those tasks could have been accomplished without guilt or negative consequences.

Tactic 15   ***Learn to recognize when you tend to procrastinate and what your procrastination activities are.***

Tactic 16   ***Recall your vision for success:*** If you have been able to portray it in a picture or drawing, post it over your workplace or where you will see it frequently. One adult student took a photograph of herself in a commencement cap and gown and posted the picture over her desk. She even made extra prints to put in conspicuous places to reinforce her good intentions.

Tactic 17   ***Follow the other strategies outlined here:*** They provide the foundation for avoiding procrastination.

Tactic 18   ***Recognize your strengths and limitations:*** Plan to accentuate the positive whenever possible and eliminate the negative, as the old song goes.

Strategy 5   ***Reward Yourself for Success***

Virtue may be its own reward, but other rewards may be even better motivators. Make a list of all the things you want to do that will give you great enjoyment and schedule them into your action plan. These enjoyable activities are excellent rewards for completing important tasks and passing milestones on your path to success. They will serve as strong motivators.

Tactic 19	***Develop a list of rewards and schedule them into your step-by-step action plan:*** Small achievements should get small rewards and big tasks should get big rewards; it's as simple as that. A small reward might be watching a favorite TV program, going out for dinner and a movie, or treating yourself to a piece of clothing that you want. The best reward for a major task well accomplished might be a weekend vacation trip, reading a new novel, or making a major purchase. Whatever you do, celebrating success brings a great feeling and a desire for renewal. Don't be afraid to toot your own horn for a job well done.
Tactic 20	***When you celebrate your successes, be sure to include others who have helped you.***
Tactic 21	***Stay on schedule:*** It's very important to get back to your scheduled tasks after your well-earned celebration. The rewards for what you've accomplished should give you the energy to renew your efforts to reach your goals.

CHAPTER 4

Six Strategies for Planning Your Major and Selecting Your Courses

Strategy 1: Find out who your advisor is and schedule an appointment

Strategy 2: Assemble your academic advising portfolio

Strategy 3: Determine the questions you should ask your advisor

Strategy 4: Develop a graduation plan

Strategy 5: Choose courses the SMART way

Strategy 6: Refine your academic plan each term

If you asked ten students on campus to define academic advising, you would get ten very different answers. Academic advising is a general term, and each student's experiences will be different. Like most aspects of college, you will get out of your academic advising experience what you put into it. To many students, academic advising means selecting and scheduling courses. While this procedure is certainly part of effective advising, a successful advising experience, for you, should be much more.

This chapter will prepare you to get the most out of your academic advising experience. Academic advising is an ongoing process and is tied closely to your personal and career goals. It is these goals that provide the foundation you need for selecting your major and scheduling your courses.

The first steps in the academic advising process are to find out who your academic advisor is and to schedule a meeting. Although this may sound simple enough, different schools have different advising delivery systems. Typically, academic advisors are either faculty members or professional advisors/counselors. In some cases you may meet first with a professional advisor, then be assigned to a faculty member for future advising. Furthermore, some schools may require proficiency testing prior to or during your first advising session. These tests will determine your readiness for college-level work and placement in foundation courses such as English and math. Your meeting with an academic advisor should take place as soon as possible to give you time to plan *before* your first term.

Strategy 1   Find Out Who Your Advisor Is and Schedule an Appointment

Advising Appointment Information

My academic advisor is ....

The office is located ....

My first appointment is ....

The test(s) I need to take are ....

....

....

Come to your meeting prepared. That way, you will make a good impression on your advisor and you will get the most out of your advising session.

Strategy 2   Assemble Your Academic Advising Portfolio

Before you meet with your academic advisor, you should put together any and all documents and records that you have. Minimally, you should bring with you:

- **Your college catalog:** Each school has a catalog of all the academic programs, policies, procedures, and course descriptions. This booklet can save you a lot of time and frustration. You should use this catalog as a working document; study it, make notes in it, and above all bring it with you to all of your advising meetings. The requirements listed in the catalog serve as your contract with the school: Read it carefully and underline important, relevant conditions.

- **Your schedule book or class bulletin:** Although you will generally receive only one college catalog for your entire college career, you will need to get a class schedule or bulletin each term or semester. Like your college catalog, your class schedule has important policies and procedures that you will be responsible for. However, because a new schedule book is printed each term or semester, you will find it has more up-to-date information. The schedule book will have an outline of important dates and deadlines, as well as information on billing and registration procedures. Of course, your schedule book will have a listing of the courses available for the term or semester and the times those courses are offered.

- **Your previous academic records:** You should not assume that your academic advisor will have all of your previous academic records. Although your advisor will usually know something about your background, no one knows as much about you as you. Therefore, be sure to have copies of your academic transcripts from any schools you have attended, as well as other credits you may have earned through work experience, advanced placement, or CLEP testing. It will also be helpful to have a portfolio of other achievements such as a resume or your military DD214.

- **All notes and documents from previous advising sessions:** You should also make sure that you save copies of any documents that you submit to or receive from the school. Be sure to make notes from every meeting you have with your advisor or other school official. When you receive information from someone, write down the person's name and when you had the conversation. All of this information can be helpful to your advisor.

- **Placement test results:** If you are required to take placement or proficiency tests, be sure to bring the results of those tests. If you have copies of any prior tests such as the ACT or SAT, bring those too.

In your first advising session, you should also be prepared to discuss your career and academic goals with your advisor. If you have clearly defined goals, be sure to share them. Your advisor may be able to recommend a program or strategy to help you achieve your goals as efficiently as possible. For example, if you are already in a well-defined career but need to complete a bachelor's degree to be promoted at work, your advisor may be able to help you identify a program to meet your goal more quickly than the route you may have chosen. Or, if you are preparing for a career change to a completely different field, your advisor may be able to develop a degree program tailored to your academic background and abilities that may be easier to achieve than the program you selected.

However, if you are unsure of your career or academic goals, *tell your advisor*. Your advisor should be able to set up a program to help you determine your goals. Most academic programs share some common requirements with all degrees. These requirements are usually called the core curriculum, basic studies, or general education requirements. Your advisor can help you identify these required courses while you are exploring your career and academic goals.

Your academic advisor should be experienced in helping students with special advising situations. If you have a special advising need, your institution may have support services available and your advisor will be able to refer you. Below is a list of special advising considerations that may apply to you. Check all items that apply to you and be sure to share them with your advisor.

❑ I am entering or returning to school because of a job change or loss.

❑ I am entering or returning to school after a divorce or loss of a spouse.

❑ I am entering or returning to school after raising a family (empty nest).

❑ I am returning to school after dropping out or stopping out.

❑ I am pursuing a specific degree to help me with a promotion or job change.

❑ I would like a degree but have no idea about a major.

❑ I am pursuing a second bachelor's degree.

❑ I am interested in taking only a few courses to upgrade specific skills (problem-solver learner).

❑ I am an adult immigrant with special needs.

❑ I would like to be a part-time, evening, or distance learner.

Strategy 3

Determine the Questions You Should Ask Your Advisor

1. What sources of alternative credit do you offer? Some examples of alternative credit are CLEP, advanced placement (AP), military, credit by individual departmental testing, credit for life or work experience (portfolio evaluation).

2. How do the credits that I have already earned fit into my program of study?

3. Is there a way for me to petition for substitutions of courses that I have already completed for other required courses?

4. Does my chosen field of study have any outside restrictions or requirements that I should be aware of? (examples include certain physical requirements for fields like nursing or police work, background investigations for law enforcement or law)

5. Does my career choice require an advanced degree or certification?

6. ....

7. ....

8. ....

Below are outlines of what should transpire during your initial academic advising session:

If You Have Specific Career and Academic Goals

- Discuss your goals
- Confirm your program of study or determine an alternative program
- Develop a program outline
- Schedule courses
- Set a follow-up meeting

If You Are Unclear about Your Career and Academic Goals

- Develop a strategy for goal identification
- Determine general education (general ed) or exploratory courses
- Schedule courses
- Set a follow-up meeting

A Special Note to Undecided Students

If you are undecided about your career goals or your choice of major, there is a lot of help available. Your advisor should be able to assist you in self-exploration exercises or refer you to someone else who can. Most schools and local libraries offer tests you can take to focus your career and academic goals. Some examples of the tests available are DISCOVER, SIGI (System of

Interactive Guidance and Instruction), MOIS (Michigan Occupational Information Survey), and Major/Minor Finder.

Once you have taken some career/academic exploration tests, you can follow up by researching the fields for which you are best suited. Some facts you should look for include the job market outlook, salary range, and educational requirements. You may also wish to conduct an information interview of professionals working in careers that interest you to find out more about them.

Strategy 4   *Develop a Graduation Plan*

Once you have identified your career and program goals, you are ready to develop a graduation plan. To do this, you and your advisor should identify your graduation requirements. Generally, your requirements will fall into one of three broad categories: (1) core requirements or general education; (2) program requirements or your major and/or minor; and (3) free electives or exploratory courses.

My program of study is ....

Core requirements	Program requirements	Free electives

Once you have determined your program requirements, you and your advisor can begin to plug in courses for which you have already received credit. Remember, this may be traditional sources of credit or nontraditional (for example, military, CLEP, AP, work experience, and so on). By doing this, you will be setting up a road map toward completion of your predetermined life and career goals.

Strategy 5   *Choose Courses the SMART Way*

S = *Select* your course load. When selecting your course load with your advisor, keep in mind that, as a rule of thumb, you should allow yourself two hours of study time for every one hour that you spend in class.

M = *Mix* of classes. If you choose to take more than one course, try to ensure you select a balanced load. Some courses may require a lot of reading and memorization, while others may require computation or writing. Some courses are taught in large lectures of several hundred students while others are smaller. If possible, try not to take all reading courses or all math courses at the same time.

A = *A's* are important. When selecting your courses, keep grades in mind. Don't overextend yourself to where you will not be able to keep good grades.

R = *Rest and relaxation*. Keep in mind that you will need to allow yourself some time for recreation. If you do not schedule breaks for yourself, you may neglect your schoolwork or other important aspects of your life to make time for needed recreation. This is only natural.

T = *Time plan*. Finally, when putting your final course schedule together, incorporate your classes into a total time-management plan.

Strategy 6   *Refine Your Academic Plan Each Term*

Because academic advising is an ongoing process, you should continue to meet with your advisor to refine your pathway to achieving your career and life goals. Although you may set an initial graduation plan and first-semester course schedule, you may need to periodically refine both your plan and your goals. For example, you may learn about alternative courses that may substitute for the requirements in your degree program. Many academic programs offer special topic courses that are only offered occasionally or are specific to current events or new developments in your field. See how these may fit into your program.

Another option may be earning academic credit through internships or cooperative education. You may be able to use your existing job for credit toward your degree. You may also be able to work an assignment in another field and earn credit while gaining valuable experience and making important contacts.

CHAPTER 5

Three Strategies for Selecting the Right Career and Getting the Job You Want

Strategy 1: Conduct a self-assessment

Strategy 2: Explore your career options

Strategy 3: Prepare for the job search

"I don't have time right now to think about my career."

"It's my first year in school. I'll look at my career choices later on."

"Plan out my career? It will be great if I can plan out next semester."

"Graduation is a long way off."

Do any of these comments sound familiar? If you're like a number of adult learners, you're back in college for job-related reasons yet actually planning out your career is the last thing on your mind. It is important to start your career planning process as early as possible. Experience has shown that the students who start the career planning process soon after starting college are more successful in getting a job after graduation, as well as being happier with their career choice and their academic experience.

Good career planning is a three-step process, consisting of self-assessment, career exploration, and job placement. When most people think of career planning, they think only of the job placement step: looking for job openings, writing and sending out resumes, and going out on interviews. In reality, the job search is a very small part of the career planning process. Successful job hunters also commit time and energy to the first two steps in the process and constantly reevaluate their career plans as they learn new things about themselves and about the world of work.

Strategy 1

Conduct a Self-Assessment

Get to know yourself! Know your strengths, your weaknesses, your abilities, your values, your interests. Until you do this, you can't possibly know what work you would be happy doing or even what you would be good at doing. Do you like peace and quiet? If yes, then you surely don't want to teach elementary school. Do you hate working with numbers? If so, you probably should rule out becoming an accountant. Do you want a job with a set schedule with weekends and evenings off? Then nursing is not for you. Even though these examples may sound ridiculous, you would be surprised how many students pick a major and a career without even looking at what the job will be like and whether it fits with their own personality.

Take a few minutes to see where you are in your own self-assessment process. Check the items below with which you agree and those with which you disagree.

Agree   Disagree

❏   ❏   I can clearly state my career goal.

❏   ❏   I have already selected my college major.

❏   ❏   I can list five strengths and five weaknesses I have.

❏   ❏   I can list five abilities or skills I would bring to a job.

❏   ❏   I can name at least five work tasks I enjoy doing.

❏   ❏   I can name at least five work tasks I do not enjoy doing.

❏   ❏   I can list at least five values that would be important to me in my job.

❏   ❏   I have defined my geographic preferences for my job.

❏   ❏   I know the salary I am willing to consider for a job.

If you agree with most of these statements, you are well on your way to knowing yourself. If there are some areas you're still not sure about, we suggest you complete the following activities. Even if you know yourself fairly well, we believe you will find them insightful and helpful. Remember, the goal here is to know everything you can about yourself. You can then use that knowledge to find a good match between yourself and a career.

Tactic 1

Start a personal career planning journal: Buy a notebook that you can use exclusively as your career planning journal. Divide the notebook into the following sections, reserving one to two pages for each heading:

Section 1:   Strengths

Section 2:   Weaknesses

Section 3:   Skills

Section 4:   Interests

Section 5:   Values

Section 6:   Classes I liked/what I liked about them

Section 7:   Classes I didn't like/what I didn't like about them

Section 8:   Job tasks I've enjoyed

Section 9:   Job tasks I've not enjoyed

Section 10: Working conditions I prefer

Take the time to fill in everything you know about yourself now under each section of your journal. As you learn new things about yourself, add to your journal. Not only will the process of keeping this journal help you to increase your self-awareness, the information in the journal can be used later to evaluate different careers you're considering.

Tactic 2   ***Ask others to share their perceptions of you:*** Talk to friends, family, teachers, co-workers, and others who know you well. Ask them to share their perceptions of you, such as strengths they see in you, things they think you do well, values they see you possessing. Add these to your journal, but make sure to note that these are perceptions of others, rather than your own.

Tactic 3   ***Visit your campus career center:*** Most campus career centers offer a number of services designed to help you during the career planning process. Some of the commonly offered services are as follows:

- Individual counseling sessions. Most centers have staff specifically trained in career counseling. These individuals can help you gain valuable insights into your values, interests, and abilities.

- Personal inventories. There are a number of inventories that you can fill out that will help you identify and describe your values, strengths, career interests, and personality traits. Most career centers administer these inventories on a regular basis.

- Personality tests. Career counselors administer a variety of personality tests that will help you during the self-assessment process. There are five types of tests (achievement, aptitude, interest, intelligence, and personality), each designed to give you different information about yourself.

If your campus does not have a career planning center, there are other ways to gather information that will help you with your career choice. Often the career counselors work out of the school's main counseling center. Check with that office to see if they have a career counselor and/or career planning materials available.

The campus library and your own community library are two other excellent sources for career planning and job search preparation materials. Most bookstores also carry a wide variety of books in this area. Although there are many good books written to help you choose a career, three books are recommended very highly by career counselors:

What Color Is Your Parachute? by Richard Bolles

Career Planning Today by C. John Powell

Super Job Search by Peter Studner

As you learn more about yourself through your visits to the career center and through taking the various tests and inventories, add this information to your journal.

Tactic 4   ***Develop your career choice evaluation matrix:*** Now that you have completed the self-assessment, it's time to develop the criteria you'll use to evaluate the various career options you'll be exploring later on. The evaluation chart you'll develop at this point can be used each time you consider a new career or even for job changes in future years.

Step 1.

Draw a chart that looks like the following. Its size will be determined by the number of items you want to evaluate for each career choice and by the number of career choices you want to evaluate.

Sample Career Choice Evaluation Matrix

Factors to consider	Job 1: nursing W X R =	Job 2: medical technology W X R =	Job 3: science teaching W X R =
1. Starting salary	2 x 2 = (4)	2 x 1 = (2)	2 x -1 = (-2)
2. Work schedule	3 x -1 = (-3)	3 x -1 = (-3)	3 x 2 = (6)
3. Travel opportunity	1 x 0 = (0)	1 x 0 = (0)	1 x 0 = (0)
4. Number of job openings	3 x 2 = (6)	3 x 1 = (3)	3 x -2 = (-6)
Total score	+7	+2	-2

Step 2.

In the left column, under "Factors to Consider," list all factors that would be important for you to consider when choosing a career. Some examples of these might be starting salary, benefits, promotional opportunities, number of job openings, work schedule, job security, travel involved, prestige, independence, level of responsibility, chance to help others, chance for creativity. You will be able to think of others that are important to you as you do some of the self-knowledge exercises. In our sample matrix, the items that were important to that particular student were starting salary, work schedule, travel opportunities, and number of job openings.

Step 3.

After compiling your list of factors, next list across the top of the chart, under each of the job headings, the careers you would like to evaluate. Our sample student, who had determined through her career search activities that she enjoyed the sciences, wanted to evaluate three careers: nursing, medical technology, and science teaching.

Step 4.

Next, assign a weight to each of your factors, under the "W" in the chart, using the following scale:

3 = The factor is extremely important to me.

2 = The factor is somewhat important to me.

1 = The factor is not very important to me.

For example, our student weighted work schedule as a 3, meaning that it was extremely important that her career have a work schedule compatible with her lifestyle.

Step 5.

For each career, assign a rating to it under "R" in the chart, using the following scale:

+2 = Greatly exceeds my requirements

+1 = Adequately meets my requirements

 0 = Not applicable

–1 = Does not adequately meet my requirements

–2 = Greatly underexceeds my requirements

In our example, in evaluating the type of work schedule in each job, the student found that nursing and medicine both were –1 whereas teaching was a +2.

Step 6.

After filling in the weights and ratings, find the score for each factor by multiplying the weight times the factor and putting it in the parentheses under each job. Then, add up each column to get a total evaluation score for each job. Notice that our student found that, overall, nursing fit best with the criteria that seemed most important.

Strategy 2   *Explore Your Career Options*

Now that you have increased your knowledge about yourself through the self-assessment process, it's time to explore your career options. As you did in the self-assessment section, take a few minutes to see where you are in the career exploration step of the career planning process. For each statement, check whether you agree or disagree with it.

Agree Disagree

❑   ❑   I can name at least five career fields that I could enter with my academic major.

❑   ❑   I can name at least ten types of employers that might consider someone with my major.

❑   ❑   I know at least ten job titles that I might consider learning more about.

❑   ❑   I know at least five resources to help me learn more about different careers.

❑   ❑   I have interviewed people working in at least two careers in which I'm interested.

❑   ❑   I already have work experience in the career field I'm considering.

These statements reflect some of the types of information you'll want to have as you determine your career options. As you gather information and

WHEEL OF FORTUNE

compare what you learn about various careers to what you've learned about yourself, you'll eventually be able to narrow down your choices to three or four viable career options on which to focus your energies. You'll want to complete this process early on so that you can select the appropriate academic major and curriculum to prepare you for your chosen career. Students who fail to complete this part of the career planning process often find themselves switching majors three or four times during their college years. We are well aware that adult learners, in particular, do not want to spend their limited time and money switching majors several times due to lack of proper career planning.

Tactic 5

Expand your personal career planning journal: Now it's time to start generating a list of careers to explore and consider. Add a new section to your journal entitled "Section 11: Career Possibilities." Start this section by doing a simple exercise. Write down any career that interests you now or has interested you in the past. Next, as you did during your self-assessment, ask others to suggest careers in which they could picture you. Add these to your journal as well.

Tactic 6

Add additional career options to your journal: There are literally thousands of occupations available; yet most people can list only a hundred or so. How many are listed in your journal so far? Probably not many! Make another visit to your campus career center and/or college library to add other careers to consider to your journal. Use the various methods below:

- Computerized career guidance programs. Most colleges subscribe to at least one computerized system such as System of Interactive Guidance and Instruction (SIGI-PLUS), Discover, Career Navigator, Career Information System (CIS), or Guidance Information System (GIS), just to name a few. By directing you through a series of exercises and inventories, these programs will then suggest a number of occupations you should explore.

- Career libraries. Most career centers have very extensive career libraries containing occupational guides, career books, salary studies, files on employers, audio-visual materials on different careers, career magazines, and journals and handouts on various occupational fields.

Tactic 7

Research the career choices listed in your journal: Once you have generated a wide variety of careers to consider, it is time to research each of them. By learning more about each career listed in your journal, you can either delete it from your list or retain it for further consideration. Some of the careers you can eliminate as soon as you read about them. You'll just know they're not right for you. For others, you may want to ask yourself the following questions:

Do I need to relocate to work in this field?

Is there an overabundance of people for this career?

Is the salary sufficient for my needs?

Do I need further schooling for this career?

These initial screening questions may help you eliminate even more careers from consideration. Ideally, through researching each career, you should end up with five to seven career fields to transfer to your Career Choice Evaluation Matrix for serious consideration.

Tactic 8   ***Conduct informational interviews:*** Reading about a career is different from observing or talking to someone who actually works in that particular field. Set up opportunities to spend time with people working in the jobs still remaining on your career possibilities list. Prepare a series of questions to ask them. Many career planning workbooks have lists of questions to ask during these informational interviews. After doing these site visits, you may be able to eliminate several more career titles from your list.

Tactic 9   ***Gain work experience in your career field(s):*** By now you have probably narrowed down your career choices and maybe even have an idea of which one or two really interest you the most. It's time to go out and try working in one of those career fields. All of the research and informational interviewing will not take the place of actually doing the job for awhile. Most colleges offer a number of career-related work experiences, either through internships, volunteering, or cooperative education programs. Check with the appropriate office on your campus that handles these types of programs.

We recognize that it is sometimes difficult for the adult learner to participate in these programs, either because of job or financial considerations. However, we encourage you to make every effort to do some kind of work experience in your chosen field. Besides testing out your career choice, the experience gives you a boost during the job search. Employers rate career-related work experience highly, often preferring to hire those candidates over ones with no experience in the field.

Strategy 3   ## Prepare for the Job Search

Hopefully, this chapter has helped you develop a plan and set of strategies for selecting a career you'll be successful at and will enjoy. Except for a few things you should do early on, the bulk of your job search preparation will not occur until your final year before graduation. You might find the following timeline helpful when you do reach this point of the career planning process.

12 Months Prior to Graduation:

- Do a co-op or internship.
- Network.
- Join professional organizations in your career field.

9 Months Prior to Graduation:

- Visit your campus career center to do the following:

    Attend a resume writing workshop.

    Attend an interview workshop.

Learn about the college's on-campus recruitment program.

Research companies to which you'd be interested in sending resumes.

- Network.

6 Months Prior to Graduation:

- Ask professors and employers to write reference letters for you.
- Have your resume reviewed and a final draft prepared.
- Prepare a cover letter.
- Sign up for any of the campus-sponsored job fairs or recruitment programs.
- Purchase an appropriate suit for interviewing.
- Set a goal: Contact ___ number of employers each week.
- Network

3 Months Prior to Graduation:

- Research companies that are interviewing you.
- Follow up with companies who have already interviewed you.
- List at least ten people who could help you with your job search.
- Get two job leads from each of the above ten people.
- Send a resume/cover letter to each job lead.
- Check job vacancy listings at your campus career center.
- Network.

Tactic 10

Network! Did you notice networking was listed on the above timeline four different times? That's because many career experts think that more jobs may be filled through networking than through any other hiring technique. The reason is simple: People prefer to hire someone they know or someone recommended by a trusted friend or colleague.

Your networking should start immediately. Get to know your professors. Get to know the career center staff. Participate in campus activities. Think of everyone you meet as part of your network. By the time you're ready to job hunt, you could easily have developed a network of 300 to 500 people. If each of them mentions your job search to two other people or lets you know about a job they heard about from any of their acquaintances, the results are obvious: There are thousands of people out there helping with your job search.

SECTION TWO

Surviving in the Learning Environment

CHAPTER 6

Three Strategies for Succeeding in the Classroom

Strategy 1: **Recognize your academic and personal strengths**

Strategy 2: **Analyze what it takes to succeed in class and on campus**

Strategy 3: **Develop a plan to accentuate your strengths in class and on campus**

If you are like most adult learners, you don't recognize many of your academic and personal strengths. Your strengths place you at a distinct advantage over younger students in class and on campus. Yet you may perceive yourself to be at a disadvantage in comparison with them.

We want you to see that you are entering a new phase of your education in a very advantageous position. To help you assess your many strengths, put checkmarks below to indicate the items with which you agree, those with which you disagree, and those about which you are unsure.

Assessing Your Strengths as an Adult Learner

Agree	Disagree	Unsure	
❏	❏	❏	Instructors like having older students in class because of their wealth of experience.
❏	❏	❏	Younger students will enjoy associating and working with me.
❏	❏	❏	My years of reading, traveling, and exposure to the world of work or child rearing will help me in the classroom.
❏	❏	❏	My reading and learning skills may actually be better than those of younger students.
❏	❏	❏	My motivation to succeed may place me at an advantage over younger students.
❏	❏	❏	My college administrators or instructors may give me credit for my past accomplishments.
❏	❏	❏	My energy and resourcefulness will enhance my ability to accomplish my educational goals.
❏	❏	❏	With so many adult learners on campus, I may be at a distinct advantage over young students.
❏	❏	❏	The communication skills I have developed will place me at an advantage in most courses.
❏	❏	❏	My ability to make decisions and handle the pressure of home- and work-related situations will help me on campus.
❏	❏	❏	The time-management skills and discipline required to manage my family or job will have a positive carry-over effect on my educational pursuits.

We want you to have a positive mind-set. If you agree with many of these comments, you are at a distinct advantage. If you don't know, that's fine. It's time for you to assess everything you have going for you.

Strategy 1   ## Recognize Your Academic and Personal Strengths

You are in a very advantageous position as an adult learner. You have many strengths, some of which you may not be aware of. We want to focus on your strengths. You should have well-founded confidence that you have so much going for you that it's time to celebrate.

Celebrate your decision to continue your education. Celebrate the circumstances under which you are entering as an adult learner. As you can see from your assessment of your strengths as an adult learner, you have a lot going for you that places you at a distinct advantage over the typical 18-year-old freshman.

Exercise   ## Assess Your Strengths

Take a few minutes to talk with someone who is close to you and with whom you feel very comfortable exchanging thoughts. Ask that person to tell you all the things he or she feels you have going for you that will help you succeed in the classroom and on campus.

We make this suggestion because adult learners need to get another person's assessment of their strengths. Most students who move right from high school into college have been receiving encouragement in their academic efforts from their instructors, friends, and parents. The adult learner usually has not had this kind of feedback for a long time.

In the space below, list your strengths as your partner in this activity has described them:

....

....

....

....

....

....

After you look at these strengths, focus on those for which you have been giving yourself credit. What are those strengths?

....

....

....

....

....

....

Now list those strengths your partner didn't mention but that you now recognize place you at an advantage:

....

....

....

....

....

....

....

We hope that this assessment of your strengths has put new wind in your sails. In the remainder of this chapter we will be pointing out some other characteristics of adult learners that will be of additional help.

Strategy 2   ### *Analyze What It Takes to Succeed in Class and on Campus*

We have focused on the often overlooked strengths you may have as an adult learner. Now we want you to analyze how you can accentuate those strengths on campus and in the classroom. What is it that admissions officers, your advisors, and most important, your instructors look for?

....

....

....

....

....

....

....

Assessing Which Behaviors Will Assist You in Class and on Campus

Put checkmarks below to indicate the statements with which you agree, those with which you disagree, and those about which you are unsure.

Agree	Disagree	Unsure	
❑	❑	❑	Instructors are threatened by challenges from an adult who may be older than they are.
❑	❑	❑	Instructors are irritated by immature and inattentive students.
❑	❑	❑	Younger students are probably less aware of how their behavior irritates instructors than are older students.
❑	❑	❑	Students are irritated by instructors who are poor communicators and unempathetic.
❑	❑	❑	Younger students are probably more likely to respond negatively to an instructor's irritating behavior.
❑	❑	❑	Arriving promptly, sitting toward the front, and paying constant attention will project a good student image.
❑	❑	❑	Asking well-thought-out questions in class will improve my learning and enhance my image.

Agree	Disagree	Unsure	
❑	❑	❑	Approaching my instructors with questions I have pertaining to class notes, readings, or assignments will be viewed positively.
❑	❑	❑	Giving instructors positive feedback in class is appropriate and mutually beneficial.

We have asked you to assess the dynamics of student-instructor interactions for two reasons. We want you to see the importance of creating a positive classroom image. Equally important, we want you to see that you have a distinct advantage over younger students.

If this exercise has helped you see the advantages you have as an adult learner, that's great. If not, by the end of the chapter you will see what an advantageous position you may actually be in. You will be well aware of the characteristics that enhance adult learners' success.

Recent studies have looked at how negative behavior by instructors affects students' behavior and vice versa. One study by psychologist Drew C. Appleby showed a clear relationship between irritating behaviors cited by both teachers and students. A student's negative behavior often leads to negative behavior on the part of the instructor, which in turn produces even more negative behavior from the student, and so on.

Five "remarkably similar pairs of behaviors" were consistently reported by students and instructors:

- Instructors are irritated by students who come to class late and students are irritated by instructors who are late.

- Instructors are irritated when students pack up their books and materials before the class is over. Students are irritated when instructors continue to lecture after a class period is over.

- Instructors are irritated by students who cut class. Students are irritated by instructors who cancel or do not show up for class.

- Instructors are irritated by students who chew gum, eat, or drink noisily during lectures. Students have similar complaints about instructors.

- Instructors are irritated by students who wear hats to class. Students are irritated by instructors who dress in a shabby or unprofessional manner.

Do these studies that focus on the impressions of younger students and their instructors have anything to say about your own interactions on campus and in the classroom? After assessing your own behavior and comparing what you are likely to do with what appears to be typical behavior of younger freshman students, you can see the advantage you have.

Adult learners act like adults in the classroom and on campus. Instructors will enjoy having you in the classroom. You will provide a model of what students are expected to do. If there is one thing on which most instructors agree, it's that adult learners make teaching a more enjoyable experience. There are characteristics typical of most adult learners that we call the adult advantage.

The Adult Advantage

Adult learners' reading skills tend to be better than younger students'. All the leisure and professional reading most adult learners have done has honed their reading skills. When we test adult learners, we typically find that they read faster and with better comprehension than younger students do. These skills pay off in the classroom. As an adult learner, you are more likely to complete reading assignments, understand the important points, and ask your instructors good questions. In essence, you will probably come to class better prepared than younger students are.

Adult learners act like adults on campus and in the classroom. Your instructors will perceive you to be more like them. With few exceptions, most instructors are more comfortable with people closer to their own age. Even if the instructor is younger than you, you'll still have an advantage. Younger instructors tend to have great respect for adult learners. Both young and older instructors typically seek out the opinions of adult learners. Your image as a more mature and knowledgeable student will place you in a position that should make attending class a pleasant and rewarding experience.

Adult learners typically are more relaxed than younger students. They have a sense of self-confidence and are interested in putting their instructors at ease. These social skills will pay off in the classroom. By communicating clearly and pleasantly with your instructors, you'll help create a classroom atmosphere that is more conducive to learning.

Adult learners are adept at letting instructors know when they have done a good job. Adults seem to have greater empathy for their instructors. When we ask adult learners how they perceive their instructors, they often tell us how difficult the task of a college instructor seems to them. Adults have empathy for what it takes to prepare for a class, stand in front of a group of students, and attempt to manage a good learning environment.

Adults are also more aware of the personal and professional demands that college professors face. Adults recognize that their instructors are often raising a family, paying a mortgage, and doing many of the same things that complicate their own lives. Perhaps it is for these reasons that adult learners often go out of their way to give their instructors some positive feedback on things they have enjoyed in class. Adults don't tend to be as patronizing as younger students sometimes are. Adults are quicker to recognize when someone has done a good job and how to go about letting them know it. After all, years of parenting and competing in the world of work forced them to learn invaluable personal skills.

Adults are excellent at asking questions to make sure they know what is and is not required of them. Instructors appreciate students' efforts to clarify their understanding of assignments. No instructor likes to see assignments turned in that are off the mark. It just creates more work for them.

Adults have a way of asking their instructors to be clear about course requirements and assignments. These questions often lead into other more casual conversations that put both parties at ease. Your questions will also convey to your instructor how serious you are about her or his class. If there's one thing that will score points, it's letting your instructor know that you value the course.

Adult learners are known for being candid and honest with their instructors. Adult learners who are late for class typically apologize or briefly explain to the instructor. Most instructors can appreciate the problems involved in balancing a job, family, and school. They understand that picking up children from day care or responsibilities at work can interfere with course attendance.

One thing that strikes us most strongly is that those irritating behaviors typical of many younger students are seldom found in adult learners. We see you as having a tremendous advantage in class and on campus. Yet, if you are like most adult learners, you haven't acknowledged your advantages. Now is the time to do so. Give yourself credit where credit is due.

Strategy 3

Develop a Plan to Accentuate Your Strengths in Class and on Campus

Put checkmarks below to indicate the statements with which you agree, those with which you disagree, and those about which you are unsure:

Agree	Disagree	Unsure	
❑	❑	❑	I will make a concerted effort to sit toward the front in each class.
❑	❑	❑	When I'm not taking notes, I will maintain eye contact with the instructor to communicate my interest in what she or he is saying.
❑	❑	❑	I will try to develop an acquaintance with several people in the class with whom I can share information and who may act as a support group.
❑	❑	❑	I will diplomatically inquire as to course and assignment requirements at any time I have the least uncertainty.
❑	❑	❑	I will develop questions before I come to class and ask for clarification when appropriate.
❑	❑	❑	If I have to be late for class or leave early, I will indicate the reason to my instructor.
❑	❑	❑	I won't burden my instructors with my personal problems. I will use the college's professional counseling, admissions, financial aid, or other support offices for advice and support.

If you agree with most of these statements, you're headed in the right direction. Developing a plan of action is fairly cut and dried. When you're in class, remind yourself of the importance of all the actions suggested above. These actions will improve your learning and enhance your instructor's teaching performance.

Adult learners face roadblocks that can sometimes hinder their performance in class. As we have suggested, most adults are excellent at informing their instructors when a particular obstacle creates an attendance problem or delays completion of a course assignment. Be frank with your instructors about these minor roadblocks, but let them know that you're aware the problems are yours and not theirs.

We caution you not to spend a lot of time discussing problems with your instructors. Some of your instructors can and will give you some very sound advice and assistance. If they are responsive and the subject is something you feel comfortable discussing, great. Go ahead and talk briefly. But it's wiser to make use of your college's professional support staff for advice on roadblocks that may be creating major problems for you.

Counseling centers for adult students are equipped with people who can deal with the problems you face. Professional counselors and the various support networks for adult learners are designed to help you develop a plan of action to remove every kind of roadblock. These people provide the best starting points in your efforts to get assistance with your transition into college and with the problems you may face along the way.

CHAPTER 7

Two Strategies for Developing Resources for Support: Learning Groups and Networks

Strategy 1: Start a learning group

Strategy 2: Develop your own learning network

There were no support groups or even any services available for us during the evening as adult students. We decided that the difference between adults and younger students was that we could do for ourselves. A couple of years ago I started a study group to help me get through my accounting class. We ended up being pretty good friends as well. It's nice to know some other people and it makes going to classes more enjoyable. I've started two other study groups since that time. You would think it's something difficult, but it's very easy. I just talk to others before class or at break, and before you know it there are so many people who want to get involved you have to have more than one group. You wonder sometimes, because this is such an important activity, why the profs don't do this in class.

I had an instructor who was a part-time teacher. He was only available immediately before and after class. So he passed out a sign-up sheet in class to identify students who would be willing to be called if others had a question or needed help. At the next class, he distributed the list. It was a real sensitive thing to do. Now I feel comfortable calling for help.

Going back to school was one of the best experiences I had. At first I thought that everyone was too busy to make new friends or had all the friends they needed. People didn't introduce themselves to me or even talk to me during class breaks. Then I decided I was the problem and I would do something about it. I started introducing myself, inviting others for a cup of coffee, asking to exchange name and phone numbers in case we needed help or missed a class. Before I knew it I was the most popular person in my class. If I only realized how much others were like me to begin with, I would have had a much easier time all along.

One of the great advantages of being an adult learner is that you probably have learned the value both of networks and of working successfully in groups. Families rely on teamwork. If you're a parent, you may coordinate activities with your spouse, children, other parents, teachers, and countless other people to make your family situation work. On the job, most people consistently work with others in groups of two or three. Successful businesses and organizations are typically team-oriented and rich with helping networks.

Adult learners generally enter college with a wealth of experience in working with family, business, and social networks. The success of these groups often hinges on sharing information and skills as well as on doing favors for one another.

Adults help each other. We have an unwritten code that says, "What's good for you is good for me. I'll help you with this today if I can count on your assistance in the future." Mothers and fathers carpool, watch one another's children, and exchange information on child rearing. Men and women assist one another on the job. The name of the game is networking—sharing, cooperation, teamwork. Everybody wins.

Strategy 1 Start a Learning Group

Groups increase your success: A learning group can be a major factor in your success and enjoyment as an adult learner. Group members tend to provide support for one another. Members perceive themselves to be working toward a common goal: everyone's success. By comparing and contrasting course notes, covering for one another when one of you can't attend class, and generally watching out for one another's interests, group members provide a rich resource for academic success.

Groups are a source of friends: Not only do groups function to supply encouragement to people who are facing similar challenges, they are also an important source of friends. Numerous studies have shown that students who have at least one other person on campus who is sincerely interested in their success have a greater potential for success than do students who are loners.

Groups give you missing information: When you think of what a group can do for you intellectually, it only makes sense that membership in a group is likely to help you do better in class and on tests. A group provides you with multiple views as to what's important. A group helps you clarify what you don't understand. If you find an instructor difficult to comprehend or inadequate, it will help you to talk with group members to assess how you might remedy the situation.

Groups save you time: By working with group members, you will usually enhance your learning for a number of reasons. Most important is that you will be exposed to multiple points of view. You will serve as consultants to one another, making it possible to reduce the amount of time necessary to determine what you should be studying, the questions you should be asking and answering, or how to go about preparing for a test. Group members can act as editors and share responsibility for assisting one another in the development of papers, projects, or routine but difficult assignments.

Groups provide encouragement: The characteristic of groups that appears to benefit adult learners most is their capacity to provide encouragement. Whether or not you have the necessary support at home or on the job, friends with whom you associate in your new learning environment can be your strongest advocates and help you toward success in good times as well as difficult ones. Friends on campus are people with whom you can share your immediate joys and your setbacks. These friends can be there to share war stories, laugh with you at what went on in class, and provide the encouragement you may need in times of stress and difficulty.

Tactic 1

Take the initiative to form your own learning group: If you believe, as we do, that having a learning group for support is desirable, then summon your energy if you need to or act upon your natural gregariousness and invite your fellow students to get involved with you and with one another.

Tactic 2

Provide leadership for the group's development: All new groups need some nurturing and direction in the beginning. Informal groups are no exception. Don't hesitate to express your thoughts about why you want a learning group and how you would like it to function. Stay flexible but make sure the group meets your needs or you will soon find it will be a nuisance rather than the support you intended.

As the group coalesces, you will find that your leadership can be shifted to other members of the group. As individuals feel more comfortable, the group will develop its own personality and members will help to share the functions that maintain it.

Strategy 2

Develop Your Own Learning Network

Just as groups are important, so are networks. In some ways, *networking* is a euphemism for "having contacts." In our context, networking implies more than having contacts; it carries with it the responsibility for deliberately planning to make your learning environment responsive to your needs for success. Although our focus is on your academic or learning environment, obviously networking is by no means limited to only one frame of reference or environment.

Tactic 3

Develop your own campus handbook: Even if you are fortunate enough to be at a school that provides a handbook or directory of services, or even an orientation program for adult learners, invest some time in checking out those areas that are important and relevant to your situation. Visit the appropriate offices and ask to meet the staff. Ask them how they can help you. Make notes especially about the people you meet, where they are located, and how you can reach them. If they are not available when you are on campus, ask whether they will see you by appointment at times convenient for you. Collecting and filing the numerous materials distributed by campus service offices will help you better understand what the campus can contribute to your success.

With very rare exceptions, the people who are in service roles enjoy being of assistance. They will welcome your interest and will want to be of help. For most of us, helping in new and different ways is a release from routine. If your approach to others is positive and open, you will have available to you all the diverse and rich resources the campus has to offer.

Tactic 4

Keep a network directory: Buy an address book that has some extra space for notations or make your own so that it can become a section in your planning organizer (see Chapter 3, Strategy 2, Tactic 10).

As you meet people on campus or those who are relevant to your learning goals, obtain their addresses and telephone numbers and make a notation of who they are and how they can be of help. Make sure you record this information for each of your instructors and others with whom you have contact throughout your college experience—office personnel, fellow students, everyone. As you meet or learn about other individuals who might serve as resources, record their names and how to contact them in the future.

This seems such an obvious thing to do that your tendency may be not to pursue it. You will be surprised, however, at how many names and details are quickly forgotten and how easily notes on scraps of paper or written inside book covers are misplaced. Having a written record of who has taught you, who has helped you, who has been a fellow student, or who may be of future help may prove to be one of the greatest assets for your continued and potential success.

Tactic 5

Keep in touch: The purpose of networking is to turn contacts into friends and supporters. The best way to do this is to keep in touch. We're not recommending contrived encounters. But if you have been helped, a brief thank-you note or phone call is appropriate and appreciated. A follow-up call or note telling how things turned out is also welcome. In today's society, thanking people is becoming a lost art, and as such is all the more valued.

And don't overlook periodic brief visits to instructors who were particularly inspiring or supportive. When it comes time to get letters of recommendation, the continuity of those relationships may determine the ease with which you can obtain strong personal references.

Call on former classmates to see how they are progressing with their plans and update them on your own developments. Keeping in touch and valuing relationships are the way friendships build and grow. We are often so busy that we forget the importance of a kind word or a friendly gesture. For most of us, it's the stuff that keeps us going.

CHAPTER 8

Three Strategies for Gaining Support from People Who Affect Your Education

Strategy 1: Recognize and acknowledge roadblocks and develop a plan of action to remove them

Strategy 2: Talk with people who can help you remove roadblocks

Strategy 3: Talk with professional people and students who have faced similar roadblocks

Whether you are continuing your education because you want a career change, need to become financially independent, or wish to reenter the job market, or for any of the other reasons people return to school, you surely envision some roadblocks.

As you contemplate taking on the obligation of continuing your education, which of the following concerns is relevant to you?

❑ Will the people around me be supportive?

❑ Can I handle the pressures of a job, family, and school?

❑ Will my family feel pleased or cheated?

❑ Will my employer encourage my educational pursuits?

❑ Will my social life be dramatically changed?

❑ Can I openly discuss my need for support and encouragement with people who can make a difference?

These uncertainties are typical of the concerns faced by most adult learners. What has surprised us time and again is that you may feel you are one of the

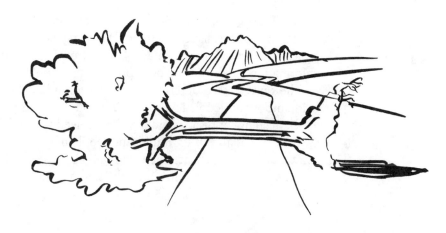

few people in this bind. We want you to see that most people continuing their education face the same roadblocks. If you are in this position, you need to know about the strategies that will help you gain the support you need to remove or bypass your roadblocks.

Strategy 1   Recognize and Acknowledge Roadblocks and Develop a Plan of Action to Remove Them

The roadblocks you face may appear overwhelming at first. We have found that once you identify exactly what they are, the next step, removing them, is much easier. To remove them you need to develop a plan of action. Your plan of action should include the following information:

Tactic 1

Describe the roadblock: Describe the roadblock you see yourself facing in as much detail as possible. Try to describe it as if you were talking to a close friend. If you have a friend who is a good listener, describe it to him or her.

Tactic 2

Determine to whom you need to talk: Ask yourself: With whom must I share my concerns? These are people who will be affected by your decisions or who can help you eliminate your roadblocks.

Tactic 3

Figure out what you need to say and how you are going to say it: You need to think out what it is people can do to help you remove a roadblock. Be able to describe exactly what it is you are asking them to do for you and why. How can they benefit by helping you? How will you try to help them?

Tactic 4

Describe the course of action you will take: Once you have talked with the people whose assistance you need, identify the most important things you must do right away to eliminate the roadblock. What are you going to do on a day-by-day basis? You want to describe your course of action in as much detail as possible.

Exercise   Removing a Roadblock

Read over the roadblocks adult students often describe to us. Then go ahead and develop an action plan for removing a roadblock you believe you face as an adult student.

A word of caution: Many of your concerns about succeeding as an adult student may be unrealistic. The roadblocks may actually be nonexistent or exaggerated. Your concerns may be based on false assumptions, inaccurate information, or a distorted perception of the problem.

The only way to determine whether a roadblock really exists is to talk with important people in your life. As you talk, you may find that the roadblock need not appear. There may be no need for a plan of action.

Your discussions with important people may prove beneficial in another way. You may find that when you talk about your concerns to important people, they may recognize the role they play in helping or hindering your success. They may feel comforted by your concern that your new role as an adult student may affect their own lives in a positive or negative way. In turn, they may offer help or advice that will alleviate many of your concerns.

Common Fears of Adult Students

- I'll never have time for my family. With a job and going back to school, I won't have time for anything else.

- I won't be able to keep up my present pace at work. Going back to school will cut into the time I use to stay ahead on my job.

- I'll resent having to give up so many of my outside interests. Taking courses will eliminate most of my social and personal time.

- My wife and children will resent my absence from home.

- My children will suffer. I've always put them first, and I can't tolerate the thought of them feeling neglected.

- I won't really fit in at college. I'll constantly feel as though people are looking at me and wondering what I'm doing there.

- My co-workers will resent it that I'm trying to get ahead and may sabotage my work at the office.

- My husband will feel threatened by my attempt to try to improve myself.

- I need a career change, but I'm afraid my wife won't support the changes it may create for us.

- I want to be in a position where I could be financially independent if something were to happen to my husband, but I don't think he'll be supportive.

Your Plan of Action

Describe your roadblock:

....

....

....

....

....

....

....

....

....

....

With whom do you need to talk?

....

....

....

....

....

....

....

....

What do you need to say and how are you going to say it?

....

....

....

....

....

....

....

....

Describe the course of action you will take:

....

....

....

....

....

....

....

....

....

Strategy 2

Talk with the People Who Can Help You Remove Your Roadblocks

Your next step is to follow the plan of action you have just described. The crucial step is talking with the people who can make a difference in your life. After you have talked with them, answer the following questions to help you assess whether your efforts appear to be worthwhile.

Yes   No

❑   ❑   I found expressing my concerns to an important person or someone close to me reduced some of my anxiety.

❑   ❑   It was helpful to look at the problem in terms of how it affected the other person. The person appreciated my concern.

❑   ❑   Writing down a plan of action to solve the problem helped me clarify what I would have to do to reduce or eliminate the roadblock.

❑   ❑   I found that the people I talked with were more supportive than I had expected.

❑   ❑   It would probably help me to talk with a professional person at the college to get some additional advice.

❑   ❑   It might be helpful to talk with other students who have faced similar roadblocks.

Strategy 3

Talk with Professional People and Students Who Have Faced Similar Roadblocks

You will often benefit from a second opinion. Your college will usually have professional counselors who are responsible for helping adult or returning students adjust to their new role.

We have found that counselors for adult learners are excited about assisting people who are returning to college. They are often people who have returned to college themselves. They have a wealth of experience advising people such as you.

Adult student counselors may suggest that you talk with other returning students. Your college may have an adult student organization that sponsors seminars, discussion groups, and a wide variety of activities to help you adjust. Just sitting and talking with other returning students will help reduce your anxiety. You will see that your problems or concerns are similar to those of other students. Equally important, you may learn of other strategies that will help remove your roadblocks.

We cannot overemphasize the value of seeking out the opinions of other returning students. The minute you get on campus, talk to the counseling staff about the professional and student support organizations that may be available to you.

SECTION THREE

Learning How to Learn

CHAPTER 9

Five Strategies for Learning Quickly and Successfully

Strategy 1: Develop a positive vision of your success

Strategy 2: Build confidence

Strategy 3: Refocus your approach to learning

Strategy 4: Develop your sense of curiosity

Strategy 5: Develop your critical thinking skills

Most of us adults approach learning within the context of our last learning experience. If you had great success as a learner in the past, you are probably quite confident and excited about again gaining mastery or proficiency and being able to demonstrate it on an exam or in a classroom discussion. If you excelled in multiple-choice questions and did poorly on essay exams, you may allow these experiences to influence your attitude toward your current situation. "Relax and enjoy this experience" may sound better than it feels. There is no question that past experiences strongly influence our present perceptions and create anticipations, fear, and uncertainty, but they also (we hope) lead to pleasure.

The fact that you're reading this book is a pretty good indication that you are preparing for and are ready for a new learning experience. One basic task that confronts you is to find out what you need to know about learning in order to do well. The following strategies will help you to assess and, if necessary, develop the learning skills that will enable you to be successful.

The first set of strategies is related to learning quickly and successfully. To determine if this is a section you should explore or skip, check the following statements. If the statement describes how you feel about yourself or is more true than false, check "Me." If the statement doesn't accurately reflect the way you tend to feel, place your check in the "Not me" column.

Me   Not me

❏   ❏   I want to study faster.

❏   ❏   I'm not sure which of my learning habits are productive and which are counterproductive.

❏   ❏   I think my learning style is often inefficient and could be replaced with a better one.

❏   ❏   I think other students are able to learn more quickly and more effectively and therefore put me at a disadvantage.

❏   ❏   I often feel that I'm not learning as much as I should.

❏   ❏   While I'm studying for a test, I'm not certain whether I'm really concentrating on the right material. By the time a final exam is given, I don't remember the material I studied for the previous tests.

❏   ❏   My study habits and ability to take exams under pressure make me nervous about competing with other students.

If you've checked "Me" for any of the above statements, you will benefit from reading this chapter. It will help you learn better, whether you are entering a college course, an executive seminar, an on-the-job training program, or a personal enrichment activity.

Most important, if you indicated that you feel insecure about your ability to learn well and compete with other people, you are among the majority. Most people feel insecure at first about their ability to compete in college or on the job. It's legitimate to feel insecure and to be insecure. It's OK to feel inadequate about your learning skills. *It's failing to overcome your feelings of inadequacy that's wrong.*

Confidence in ourselves is so important for our success! When we're anxious about a situation, most of us don't remember how many times we've already succeeded. The fact that we've survived up to this point in our lives puts us way ahead. We're not at the beginning anymore—we're well on our way to more successes.

Confidence in ourselves and feelings of inadequacy are twin forces that exist simultaneously in most of us. The dynamic tension between the two sets of forces is what propels us through life, helping us decide the things we will do and those we will avoid. Most of our concerns about our inadequacies grow out of our fears of looking stupid or silly if we fail and of being seen as an impostor if we succeed.

It's difficult to change lifetime patterns. Our purpose in exploring this theme is to make sure you realize how natural and typical your feelings are. Taking risks is an important activity for us all. It's how we handle the outcomes of risk taking that makes the difference. Knowing that others have walked down the path we are on now and have been nervous about their experience ought to bring some comfort. Knowing that many of the people we meet along the way want to be helpful and will sustain us in our efforts is even more important. The element that's critical for our success is our confidence that things will work out and our willingness to ask for help when we need it. Willingness to ask for help is our most important asset in our journey and is essential to counterbalance and overcome feelings of inadequacy. Ultimately the confidence we need will come from our successes—small at first and bigger and more impressive as we go on. There is some truth to the old saying that "Nothing succeeds like success." You can help yourself be successful by developing a positive vision of your success. Seeing yourself as successful, writing down what your success will mean, or even drawing a picture of your success will help you create a pathway to it.

Strategy 1   *Develop a Positive Vision of Your Success*

In our work with adult learners, we have suggested drawing a picture of a grade report with the grade you are willing to work for prominently visible, or even to take a picture of yourself in a commencement cap and gown. Some students write down the title of the new job they're aiming for or the new salary they expect to earn as a result of their learning experience. Post this vision of success in a prominent place that you can see easily and often. Remember the student who placed her "graduation" picture on her desk to inspire her to stick with it in good as well as difficult times.

Strategy 2   *Build Confidence*

Confidence is an essential ingredient of your success. The more you succeed, the more confidence you will build and the more assertive you will become in exploring additional earning opportunities for your growth and development.

When your confidence is tested by extensive demands, think about all of the times you have been successful and how you achieved that success. Think about your current situation. Draw a vertical line down the center of a sheet of paper. On the left half write what you see as the strengths that will promote your success. On the other half write what you see as the elements that create your nervousness, uncertainty, concern, or whatever you call your reasons for possible failure. Review each strength and think about all the ways you have used this strength in the past to overcome difficulties. As you review each of your strengths, jot down your positive action steps. Now look at your reasons for concern and list all the things you can do to overcome them. Draw on your past successful experiences and think about new approaches as well. At all times, keep your vision of success prominently in view. If it's worthwhile to strive for success, you can take this second step of building the confidence that will enable you to achieve it.

Strategy 3   *Refocus Your Approach to Learning*

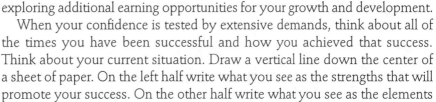

To be a more successful learner, you need first to analyze your learning style in order to build on your strengths and refine them. What are you already doing well? What few learning strategies do you need to change?

Practice refocusing—that is, refining—your approach to learning. Start where you are and refocus your approach. Knowing what to change in your learning style and mastering new skills are important. Check off the characteristics below that resemble the way you approach learning, whether in class, on the job, or at home.

❏ I quickly scan most reading material—magazine articles, newspapers, reports, textbook chapters—looking for the important information.

❏ I try to read most information rapidly to get the big picture.

❏ I'm not afraid to ask questions about what I'm learning or seek clarification if I don't understand the instructor's assignments or what I'm reading.

❏ As I read, when I come to information I want to remember, I slow down and think it through.

❏ When I attend meetings, I take notes on the most important points.

❏ I anticipate questions I could be asked about the material I'm reading.

❏ When possible, I get copies of old tests to see whether questions that were asked in the past are similar to those I think might be on my test.

❏ I use a schedule, checklist, or calendar to remind myself of important events and when tasks are due.

❏ I assign priorities to the tasks I have to complete and work to do them in the order I have indicated.

❏ When I listen to people speak, I think about the points they are making, whether or not I agree, and which of the points I should remember.

❏ I search out others to discuss my learning with them.

If you checked off most of the above points, you probably don't need to make major changes in your learning style. Most likely, you simply need to refocus it. You didn't get where you are today because you've failed as a learner. You are probably very successful, but at times inefficient.

You may have checked off few or none of the above statements. You may have strong evidence to suggest that if you are to compete successfully, you will need additional help in learning, reading, writing, and computational skills. But before you decide you need to make a major change, read through this chapter and the chapters that follow on learning, reading, and preparing for tests. We often find that people who initially think they are in need of significant change need far less assistance than they predicted. If after you've completed the following chapters you still feel you need more help, then go ahead and seek assistance from a professional person on campus. Most colleges have a reading and learning skills center with a professional staff who provide individualized and group instruction in these areas.

Strategy 4　　**Develop Your Sense of Curiosity**

Asking questions is the key to learning success!

The most important key to learning is the ability to formulate hooks onto which to hang the information you are processing. The best hooks are the questions you can generate about the topics you are studying. Think about the task of asking questions. To many people it seems silly. Many adult students indicate that asking questions doesn't come naturally or easily.

Every research experiment begins with a question the researcher asks about the topic under investigation. Authors of textbooks start by identifying the questions that will need to be answered if their book is to cover all of the relevant material.

Questions provide the impetus as well as the framework for reports we are asked to write and for speeches we need to give. Questions determine the foundation and framework for learning. They are the basis of curiosity and the hooks on which we hang our new learning and organize what we already know.

If questions are such an important tool in the learning process, why do we have so much difficulty formulating them? And when they do surface in our minds, why do we feel so uncomfortable about asking them?

Young children ask questions naturally, and many of them drive their parents crazy in the process. Some children learn in time that their parents or caregivers really don't have the time, energy, or patience to answer all their questions. Eventually these children come to feel uncomfortable about asking questions and stop doing it.

When these children get to school, the same thing sometimes happens all over again. The teacher doesn't have time. "You're asking too many questions. Wait till later. This isn't the right time. We'll get to that later."

We're even taught to laugh at people who ask questions. We learn that there are dumb questions, inappropriate questions, and soon we stop asking. Unfortunately, we stop asking questions not only in the classroom but everywhere else.

These inhibitions carry right over from school into our adult life. In higher education and in our work, we learn to feel that asking questions will make us look inadequate or incompetent. These inhibitions extend to asking for help.

Look at how these inhibitions carry over into our behavior as consumers. When we shop for new products, we often don't make the effort to think of questions to ask salespeople. If we do have questions, we are often reluctant to ask them. We feel we are taking up too much of the salesperson's time.

Asking questions is the key to learning quickly and successfully!

Strategy 5　　**Develop Your Critical Thinking Skills**

Much has been written about the importance of critical thinking and teaching people how to be critical thinkers. Although there is little consistency in the way experts define the concept, there is general agreement that critical thinkers ask and answer a lot of questions both in the privacy of their own thoughts and overtly in class and on the job.

Are you a critical thinker? Do you ask important questions and seek their answers? How you pose questions, the types of questions you develop, the quality of the questions, and the amount and type of information you get from your questions may vary. For most people these factors are a result of the models they have had in their upbringing and in school.

If the models you had as a child at home and in school encouraged you to ask questions and seek answers, you probably learned to be a critical thinker. You learned to question the information placed before you. You asked, "Is the information accurate? What does the information tell me that I need to know or would like to know?"

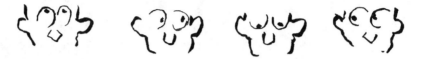

If your parents or teachers discouraged you from asking questions, you now probably ask fewer questions than it would be to your advantage to ask. As you observe the people about you, you will see many who seldom ask questions. They seem to go about their business, complying with what other people ask of them. These people do what authority figures tell them to do.

Chances are that you ask a lot of questions and go to great lengths to seek the answers. You question what you hear from speakers in classes, on television, and on the job. You have learned to be skeptical. You focus on sources of information that are reliable. You avoid listening to people who appear to have little knowledge.

You may be fascinated by people who see the world very differently from the way you do. Clearly their ideas and philosophies are very different from your own. But you value listening to people whose thoughts, though different, may dramatically enhance your own. You are looking for insight, even though it may conflict with your present mind-set.

Critical thinkers, then, are people who ask a lot of questions and are willing to look at all sources of credible information. They don't let people stifle them when they seek the truth. Critical thinkers want to look at the world from a wide variety of perspectives, knowing full well that the way they see the world tomorrow may contradict the way they see the world today.

So if you want to be a critical thinker, you must always be willing to ask questions constantly and to look at many alternative answers. Only when you have sorted out the sense from the nonsense can you be confident that you have truly done yourself justice.

You might find it of interest that at a recent meeting of many of the world's leading authorities on intelligence, there was one clear area of agreement. These scholars agreed that intelligent people consistently ask many questions. Equally important, intelligent people look for as many answers as possible before coming to a conclusion.

What do you need to do, then, to become a truly critical thinker? Ask as many questions as possible. Look at all the alternatives. Evaluate your answers from every useful perspective. Then be willing to acknowledge that your answer may very well change as a result of new information. By always being open and evaluating new viewpoints, you position yourself to think critically and to develop your intelligence.

Is Questioning the Key to My Success?

Respond to the following statements to consolidate your feelings about what your next steps should be in becoming a more successful learner. Indicate whether you agree, disagree, or are unsure by checking the appropriate box.

Agree Disagree Unsure

❏ ❏ ❏ To do well on tests, I have to answer questions successfully.

❏ ❏ ❏ Most authors write books that focus on questions the authors believe are important.

❏ ❏ ❏ Most speakers I listen to are trying to convince me that they have answers to important questions.

❏ ❏ ❏ Involvement in scientific research is a quest for answers to questions.

❏ ❏ ❏ Inventions and innovations are products of asking questions.

❏ ❏ ❏ The notes I take during lectures or presentations could be turned into questions and answers.

❏ ❏ ❏ The most intelligent people I know are people who can answer the questions important to their line of work or general interests.

❏ ❏ ❏ People who succeed on their jobs are typically people who can answer important questions for their boss and for the people they supervise.

❏ ❏ ❏ Groups of students working together can typically predict most of the questions that will appear on their exams.

❏ ❏ ❏ I could save a lot of time by focusing my reading, note taking, and preparation for exams on developing answers to questions I believe are important.

We want you to feel comfortable, confident, and excited about the concept that the key to learning quickly and successfully is asking questions.

American business and industry have begun to recognize the importance of getting their employees involved in team efforts to ask questions and find answers that will move them ahead of their foreign competitors. Television commercials for a major corporation, for example, made excellent use of getting people excited over asking questions anytime, anywhere. Bright corporate executives are seen in a variety of situations—taking a shower, sitting on the beach, involved in deep thought. As they are thinking, an interesting possibility comes to mind. The executive rushes to the phone and calls a colleague. In a burst of enthusiasm he exclaims, "What if . . . ?"

As you think of this commercial and the material you just read, do you say any of the following to yourself?

Yes   No

❑   ❑   Do I ask enough questions?

❑   ❑   Am I inhibited about asking questions?

❑   ❑   Would I be viewed as more enthusiastic in my work if I asked more questions?

❑   ❑   Would I be happier if I directed more of my life to getting answers to questions I feel are important?

❑   ❑   Would I be happier on my job if I spent more time looking for answers to questions?

❑   ❑   Would my learning be more focused if I directed more of my effort toward seeking answers to questions?

❑   ❑   Would I feel more creative if I asked more questions?

There is something contagious about wanting to be actively looking for new solutions and answers to questions. If you were discouraged from asking questions as a child, it's time to renew that curiosity in yourself. If you accept that challenge, then you are ready to try a few learning strategies that will give you a whole new feeling of excitement about learning.

CHAPTER 10

Five Strategies for Reading Quickly and Successfully

Strategy 1: Ask questions before you read

Strategy 2: Determine and document where the questions are answered

Strategy 3: Understand what the answers are by reading the material

Strategy 4: Learn the answers by reciting them and even writing them out

Strategy 5: Test yourself

Which of the following statements about reading are true?

- ❏ I should read most material at the same speed.
- ❏ Underlining important information as I read will help me remember it.
- ❏ Good readers can remember most of what they read.
- ❏ Reading slowly is the key to good comprehension.
- ❏ Good readers try to memorize large amounts of information as they read.
- ❏ When I read rapidly I remember less information than when I read slowly.

If you believe most of these statements to be true, this chapter should help you become a better reader and save you a lot of time.

Exercise

Assessing Your Reading Style

Here is a test to help you focus on the key strategies for efficient and effective reading. Pick out a book you are using on the job, a book you are reading for your own professional or personal growth, or a text you are reading for a college course. Now pick out a chapter you would like to read.

As you look over the chapter, think about the most efficient and effective procedures you could use to read and remember this chapter. If you're like most people, you haven't given much thought to the steps you follow when you read and attempt to remember information. Now is the time to give it serious thought. In the following space, describe the steps you would follow in reading this chapter. Then describe what you would do after reading the chapter to help you remember what you read.

Steps in Reading My Chapter

1. ....
2. ....
3. ....
4. ....
5. ....

Strategies for Remembering My Chapter

1. ....
2. ....
3. ....
4. ....
5. ....

Which of the following statements are true about the way you approached reading and remembering your chapter?

❑ One thing that came to mind as I looked over the chapter was: "What questions does this chapter answer?"

❑ Before reading the chapter, I decided to survey it. I wanted to see if there were any clues to the important questions answered in the chapter, such as a list of questions at the end or a summary.

❑ I decided to read through the chapter quickly looking for answers to the questions I wanted to answer.

❑ As I read, I slowed down when I came to information I wanted to be sure I remembered. I read more rapidly through information I felt was less important.

❑ As I read, I looked for terms and concepts I thought were important.

❑ As I read, I stopped and wrote down questions I found were answered in the chapter that I felt were important.

❑ After reading, I tried to answer the questions I believed were important by thinking them through. I even wrote out the answers to the most important questions.

❑ If I had to take a test about the chapter, I would practice answering the questions I had developed as I read the chapter.

If your strategy for reading and remembering included many of these tactics, you are probably a very good reader. Even so, it will benefit you to skim through the remainder of this chapter very rapidly to pick up a few pointers.

If you didn't include many of the tactics indicated above in your strategy, this chapter could dramatically change the way you read and save you considerable time. A reading strategy used by many good readers is the ADULT method.

The ADULT Method of Reading

ADULT is an acronym that represents the five strategies successful readers and learners typically adopt:

A *Ask* questions before you read.

D *Determine* and document where the questions are answered.

U *Understand* what the answers are by reading the material.

L *Learn* the answers by reciting and even writing them out.

T *Test* yourself.

The strategies of the ADULT method of reading are really very simple. Good students figure out what questions are *answered* in the chapter. They read quickly to *determine* and document where the answers to those questions are located. As they read, they formulate an *understanding* of what good answers to the questions look like. After reading, they *learn* the answers by reciting and writing out answers to the questions. They *test* themselves with the questions and answers they have developed to consolidate their learning.

Read a Textbook Using the ADULT Method

It's important for you now to use the ADULT method with a textbook or a professional book, something other than leisure reading. The best approach is to use the chapter you selected for the previous exercise. Let's walk through the ADULT method to master the chapter you have chosen.

Strategy 1   Ask Questions Before You Read

Your best sources of questions are typically questions at the end of the chapter, a chapter summary, or a list of objectives at the beginning of the chapter. If you find any of these elements, read them right away.

Now return to the first page of the chapter. Survey the chapter by looking for other sources of questions. You want to look at what we call study aids: headings, subheads, pictures, tables, illustrations, italicized and boldface words, and definitions in the margins. The study aids should stimulate your mind to develop questions.

Developing questions is not meant to be a long, drawn-out process. Developing questions by reading a summary, looking over a list of questions, or surveying a chapter shouldn't take you more than a few minutes. You should then have formulated at least five to ten questions that you think your instructor is likely to ask you about this chapter.

You don't want to overload yourself with too many questions before you start reading. You simply want direction. No one can predict all the important questions that will be answered. Nor should you be worried about it. A few solid questions will give you the focus you need before you start reading. So review your questions and recast them into a few carefully developed ones that will guide your studying.

Now try Strategy 1 with your chapter!

Strategy 2   ### Determine and Document Where the Questions Are Answered

When you have formulated a few well-focused questions, you can read rapidly, looking for the answers. As you read, you will be documenting for yourself that these or other important questions are actually answered in the chapter. If you have too many questions, you will feel overwhelmed. By reading to find the answers to a few solid questions, you will get a good grasp of the chapter. You should be able to summarize the main points of the chapter after a first reading.

If, after reading the chapter, you feel you have missed answers to important questions, you can quickly go back and get them. But your initial goal is to get through the chapter at a comfortable pace and to be able to summarize it. You should not expect a complete understanding of the chapter the first time through.

You may be saying to yourself, "But I can't afford to miss a thing in the chapter. I have to read slowly to make sure I totally understand everything!" This is a typical concern. But be realistic. Most instructors and supervisors want you to understand the major concepts. You need to have the "big picture." If you know that you'll be required to have in-depth and detailed knowledge of the material, you'll need to read through it a second time, and perhaps a third, looking for and documenting these specific concepts in notes or outline form.

You may also be worried that you won't predict the same questions that your instructor will ask on an exam. To reduce your uncertainty, be assertive and discuss your questions with other students in the class. Even better, ask your instructor if your questions cover the information about which you'll be tested.

The critical idea for you to understand is that the purpose of your first reading of a chapter, regardless of the content, is to get the big picture. If you know you'll need more information, you can go back and get it. But you don't want to memorize everything said in every chapter. That's an inefficient learning strategy.

Strategy 3   ### Understand What the Answers Are by Reading the Material

Having asked the questions (Strategy 1), you will read rapidly, focusing on finding answers to your questions. As you read, additional information pertaining to your questions will often pop off the page at you. Your brain will say, "Aha! There's some more information that can help answer my question."

Slow down and look over this information. Work the information around into your own words and phrases so that they form an answer that makes sense to you. Essentially you talk to yourself until you understand what a good answer sounds like.

Don't automatically discard material because it doesn't fit your preliminary model. If you find a lot of material on a topic that you didn't anticipate, you may need to add additional questions to your list.

At this point, many readers use an alternative strategy that is a major mistake. Rather than carrying on a conversation with themselves and formulating an answer, they simply underline the information or mark it with a highlighter. This doesn't help you develop an understanding of information. It actually does just the opposite. It gets the mind to relax, to feel the learning task has been brought to resolution. After all, there's no need to deal with this now—it's highlighted for future reference.

To make sure you understand the answer to one of your questions, write the answer out in your own words, stated in such a way that you won't forget it. It will then be an answer that you will be able to explain to someone else and feel comfortable putting on your test. When you understand the material well enough to put it in your own words, you have mastered it. Memorizing isn't mastering.

If information is to become meaningful to you, you must rework it in your own words. If you want to *understand* information, formulate answers that make sense to you. Don't try to memorize what the author said.

After you have reformulated information in an understandable answer, start reading again. Read rapidly until you find an answer to another important question. As you can see, you're never reading at a uniform rate. You read rapidly to find answers to questions. You slow down when you come to information that answers a question. You formulate an *understandable answer* and you move on.

One word of caution: Some of you may be saying, "These strategies for reading apply to textbooks or narrative texts. But this won't work on classical literature, fiction, or math and science books." Yes and no.

Understanding literature and fiction requires us to comprehend more than the main points and supporting points. The ADULT method addresses this concern. The ADULT method provides you with strategies that allow you to move quickly through all material, including the heaviest reading. You will then have time to ponder the issues and questions that readers of classical literature and fiction like to address. But if you don't have a method that allows you to read such material efficiently and effectively, you won't have time to ponder anything other than why you're not getting through your reading.

Math, physics, chemistry, and science materials often fool students. The key to understanding these books is problem solving. You master the concepts in these books by following the examples of problem solving found in each chapter. When you assess the types of problems you should be able to solve, you will spend most of your time using the models in these books as you work through the problems presented throughout the chapters or at the end.

Now try Strategies 2 and 3 with your chapter!

Strategy 4   *Learn the Answers by Reciting Them and Even Writing Them Out*

You are now in a position to put yourself at ease. Having read the chapter or instructional unit and formulated answers to questions, you now need to make a decision. Of all the questions you answered, which are you most likely to be tested on or asked to answer? Which answers do you want to make sure you retain for your own satisfaction?

Whether you have to be able to answer questions for other people or for yourself, now is the time to decide which answers you'll make further effort to retain. You can either write or talk out answers to your questions. We suggest you do both. If you have written out some of the answers while you were reading (Strategy 3), you are already ahead of the game. If not, now is the time to do so.

Talking out an answer makes writing out the same answer easier. When you hear aloud what you are thinking, you often clarify important points. As you talk out your answers, you automatically prove to yourself that you truly know them.

By writing out answers, you provide yourself with several benefits. You have written answers you can use when you prepare for tests. When you write answers you practice the exact behavior required of you in most testing situations.

Too often learners try to retain information by simply flipping through the pages and talking to themselves about the major concepts of a chapter. There are several problems with this approach. An obvious problem is that you will never take a test in which you are asked to sit down with your book and talk through the answers. A supervisor or instructor will expect you to write answers to questions.

An additional problem is that when people talk themselves through answers, they often do the talking silently, inside their heads. As we think through things, many of us are in the habit of saying to ourselves, "I know the answer to that." Or we talk through an incomplete answer. There is no better way to find out whether you really know an answer than to write it.

Now try Strategy 4 with your chapter!

Strategy 5   *Test Yourself*

Your preparation for an exam should now have changed radically. If you are in possession of questions and answers you have developed, your review will focus on the answers to your questions.

This is an excellent time to work in a study group. Sharing questions and answers and testing one another are two of the best ways to demonstrate to yourself that you have really mastered the material. Studying with others at this point helps you see what you may have missed. Your mind is anxious to accept and retain additional information that will prepare you to be successful on the exam.

Your preparation will not consist of rereading chapters or trying to memorize notes. You practice the exact behavior expected of you, asking and answering questions.

The ADULT method of reading will be a real key to your efficiency and effectiveness as a learner. We typically find that many learners have developed inefficient reading habits that are based on misinformation. We don't want this misinformation to prevent you from changing over to the ADULT method.

Now try Strategy 5 with your chapter!

Consideration 1

If I don't read slowly, I won't be able to learn everything I need to retain.

The assumption on which this notion is based is that if you allow your eyes to drift slowly over the words, the information is more likely to be absorbed into your brain and thoroughly processed. In contrast, if you go too rapidly, your brain can't process each word. Therefore, you will miss some information that you might need to remember.

The fallacy here is the idea that you can remember almost everything over which your eyeballs pass and that your brain is capable of remembering what you have read word for word.

If you really believe that by reading slowly you will remember what is on a page in great detail, try the following test:

Read slowly and destroy a myth!

Take any traditional book and read page 150 or a page nearby very slowly. Take five minutes or ten, whatever you need. Now close the book. Take a sheet of paper and write word for word what you just read.

We pose this problem to you for one reason. It's very important for you to see that when you read, you don't remember things word for word, or even close to it. What, then, do you remember?

First let's talk about what you don't remember. Typically you don't remember anything word for word unless you deliberately memorize it. Nor do you need or want to. Your brain is geared to pick up meaningful information as you read. You optimize your brain's ability to pick up meaningful information by formulating questions you want to answer before you read. You then read to answer the questions.

Next time you're sitting around with a group of friends, ask them if they can remember word for word any page of any book they have read recently. Most people don't practice memorizing what they read.

You'll find that no one will be able to remember a specific page word for word. Next, ask them to summarize what they read on a specific page. No one will be able to do that, either. Now ask, "Can someone describe the  major ideas that are discussed around a specific page?" If you're lucky, you may find someone who can summarize the major ideas that are discussed in that portion of the book. Each idea that comes to mind acts as a reminder of another important point, and so on until the person has presented a summary of the material.

This exercise will help you and your friends see how your memory works. You read and remember meaningful information, answers to questions. You summarize the material you have read by piecing the information together.

This is a simplistic description of human information processing and memory. Our main concern is that you not get trapped into the superstitious belief that reading slowly will help you understand information more clearly and remember more of what you have read. You can't remember everything you read, and you shouldn't try. What you want to do is develop efficient and effective strategies that will help you learn the meaningful information, the answers to important questions, as fast as possible. The ADULT method is designed for this purpose.

Consideration 2

If I read rapidly, I won't be able to remember what I read!

There is an optimum speed at which you want to read. Reading slowly doesn't enhance your understanding if you don't know what you are looking for. Reading slowly and aimlessly just helps you fall asleep. Typically, if you read too slowly, your brain doesn't pick up the meaningful information you want to understand and remember.

Research in reading and perception has shown that if you direct your reading, which boils down to figuring out what questions you want to answer, you are better off reading rapidly.

You may ask, "Why shouldn't I read slowly, looking for answers to questions?" One can only speculate as to what's going on in your brain as you read. It's likely that when you figure out what you want from your reading, you become goal-oriented. You are in pursuit of some rewards. The faster you get those rewards, the happier you will be. Those rewards are the answers to your questions.

Consider this example. Let's say your boss comes to you and says, "Get the answers to these questions within an hour. It may cost us a lot of money if you don't!"

You have several sources of information that can supply you with the answers you need. You scan the sources rapidly, looking for the answers. Each time you find an answer, your brain goes "Aha!" You're excited. You're getting the information you need. The faster you go, the more excited you get. When you get stalled because you can't find an answer, you get anxious. Now you find the answer and you get excited again. The process goes on and on.

There is an optimum speed at which you can read different types of materials. You can determine that speed by practicing reading more rapidly in search of the answers to your questions. If you increase your speed and continue to find the answers you need, then you are at an efficient and effective speed.

The other benefit of reading rapidly as you look for answers is that you keep active and alert. Your brain is stimulated as you find answers. You feel you are learning, and that's the name of the game!

Assess your thoughts about changing your reading strategy.

Yes No

❏ ❏ I feel I could apply the ADULT method to most books.

❏ ❏ I now see that reading slowly may not be to my advantage.

❏ ❏ I feel I could read faster looking for answers to questions without hurting my comprehension.

❏ ❏ I am now more certain that my reading should be focused on searching for answers to my questions.

If you feel comfortable with the ADULT method, it's time to look at how you would apply it to the two other types of reading most adult learners face: (1) professional magazines and journals and (2) works of fiction and general nonfiction. The ADULT method can be easily adapted to both categories of reading.

Reading Professional Magazines and Journals

The articles in professional magazines and journals are intended to convey important information to readers with advanced training and expertise. When students read these essays, the writing style and format often leave them struggling to grasp even the main points. You can use the ADULT method to learn what you need quickly, without wasting a lot of time.

The ADULT formula for reading professional magazines and journals is:

A: By reading the abstract or summary of the article first, you can determine which questions are addressed in the article. You will also get a brief description of the answers to those questions.

You may want to stop here. If you just need an overview of what is being said, the summary or abstract may be sufficient. If you are unsure, go on to the next steps.

D and **U:** Read the introduction and body of the article, seeking answers to questions that are not provided in the summary or abstract. This step may also provide you with a more complete understanding of the questions that were answered in the abstract or summary.

At this stage, we caution you to assess whether you need only a brief overview of the main points the author is raising or an in-depth understanding. We are not trying to discourage you from reading an article in depth. If necessary, do so. We simply don't want you to waste your time. Too often learners tell us, "All I needed to do was get a quick summary of the article!" after they have spent an hour laboring over unneeded detail.

L and **T:** To prove to yourself that you can summarize the main points of an article, either talk out or write out a short summary of what the article has told you. If you are going to be responsible for comparing and contrasting information found in several articles, your summary of each article will provide you with an easy mechanism for review.

For college students, summaries of articles are especially helpful at test time. Rather than reread journal articles, all you have to do is review the summaries you have produced.

Reading Fiction and General Nonfiction

Works of fiction and general nonfiction may appear less suitable to the ADULT method. After all, where do you find study aids that highlight the important questions? Here is the way to apply the ADULT method to these books.

A: Survey the book by reading the front, back, and inside of the jacket to determine the major issues raised in the book. Once you have done a quick survey to determine the focus of the book, you should have a few basic questions, such as:

- Who are the main characters in the story and what is their relationship?

- Is there a major theme running through the story?

- What important events occur and how are they interrelated?

Your next step is to skim through the book, looking for study aids that pinpoint more detailed questions. If there is a table of contents, the information here can be turned into questions. At a minimum, you should be able to use chapter heads and subheads to develop your more detailed questions. Skimming should take you five to ten minutes.

D and **U:** By skimming through the book, you will determine where the questions are answered. Now you simply begin reading to see if you have accurately predicted the direction in which the book is headed. By the time you get through the first chapter, you should have an adequate feel as to whether your questions have given you the proper focus or whether you need to refocus your reading.

L: As you complete each chapter, you prove to yourself that you can answer the important questions in the chapter by summarizing for yourself what you have read. Writing a short paragraph after each chapter will take about two minutes. When these short summaries are combined, the typical result is about a two- to three-page summary of the book.

T: If you should be tested on this material, you'll be in good shape. To prepare for the test, you'll use your summaries to refresh your memory. Your summaries will contain the answers to the questions on which you're likely to be tested.

You'll compare and contrast your summaries of various books to see how they are interrelated. This process will give you a feel for the type of essay questions that require you to integrate material from several sources.

The End Product

The end product of your reading should be a developed ability to summarize the book and answer questions about it, some of which your instructor or supervisor expect you to answer. Questions that often appear on exams on readings of fiction and nonfiction look like this:

Summarize the major points raised by _____ in her book _____ as related to the issue of _____.

Compare and contrast the arguments that _____ raises in his book _____ with those of _____ in her book _____.

Identify the similarities and differences in the theories of _____ and _____ and the implications of these theories in respect to _____.

We have discussed in great detail how to use the ADULT method to enhance your ability to read faster and maintain a solid understanding of what you read. In Chapter 11 you will learn strategies for listening and note taking. Once you have integrated your reading strategies with those for listening and note taking, you will be in superb shape to focus on the remaining activities required to be a successful learner—preparing for and taking tests.

Exercise   *Apply the ADULT Method to a Book*

This exercise is an excellent way to apply the ADULT method of reading to a book of your choice. When you practice using the ADULT method to read a book in class, you can compare and contrast the results you get by using the five ADULT strategies with the results obtained by your friends.

This is a useful exercise because it helps you see that the ADULT method is simple and applicable to many types of texts. Although you may take two class sessions to complete the exercise on one chapter, you will see that without interruptions, several valuable things will happen when you have finished using the ADULT method.

- You will have read with a focus.

- You will know how to read more rapidly.

- You will feel you have accomplished something useful while you read: You have answered questions.

- You will have clear answers to questions and feel prepared to take a test on the chapter.

1. First review the ADULT method. The goal is to familiarize yourself with the five strategies you will follow in reading a text chapter.

2. Once everyone is familiar with the five strategies of the ADULT method, follow the five strategies as you read a text chapter. After the class has completed each strategy, members of the class should describe what they have done. This activity ensures that all of you see what is being asked of you as you apply each strategy to the text.

3. When the class has finished this exercise, each person should now be familiar with the ADULT method and be able to describe how to apply it to any text. A good summary exercise is to write out an explanation of the ADULT method and describe how to use the five strategies to read a chapter.

CHAPTER 11

Five Strategies for Listening and Taking Notes

Strategy 1: Determine what you want from a lecture or meeting

Strategy 2: Keep track of what is said

Strategy 3: Develop outlines to record information

Strategy 4: Refine your material and integrate it with other information

Strategy 5: Use the ADULT method to develop useful notes

The listening and note-taking strategies of successful adult learners have a similar pattern. We have listed many of the keys to their success. How does your approach match theirs?

Check the following statements that are true of you:

❏ As I listen to speakers, I listen for statements with which I agree or disagree.

❏ As I listen to speakers, I make comments to myself regarding important things they have said.

❏ When I attend a lecture, presentation, or business meeting, I try to figure out what questions the speakers are likely to answer and I listen for those answers.

❏ As I take notes, I try to organize the information into meaningful statements.

❏ I perceive most lectures as similar to chapters in books. They are loaded with answers to questions.

❏ After taking notes on a lecture or a meeting or a book, I write out questions I believe were answered. I then rework my notes into a meaningful set of questions and answers.

❏ When I study my notes, I don't try to memorize them. Rather, I try to remember the information by quizzing myself on questions I develop from the notes.

❏ I regularly exchange notes with other people to see what information they have captured that I did not.

❏ I work in study groups in which we develop possible test questions from our notes.

❏ I feel free to show my notes to my instructors to see if they believe I am focusing on the important concepts.

❑ When I find that certain questions have been only partially answered by my notes, I check other sources such as texts, articles, and friends to find the necessary information.

These statements offer important clues to successful listening and note taking. The next few pages are filled with strategies that should make a big difference in the way you approach listening and note taking.

Which of the following problems do you face when you listen to speakers and take notes?

❑ I often have a hard time determining what is most important and should be written down.

❑ I often lose my train of thought.

❑ I find myself drifting off or feel drowsiness coming on.

❑ I keep wondering when the meeting or lecture will be over and find myself looking at my watch.

❑ The notes I take don't seem to have much use after the lecture or meeting or book is over.

❑ I have difficulty using my notes in a helpful way, such as preparing a report or studying for a test.

❑ I find myself wanting to skip lectures or meetings that I think will be boring.

If these statements reflect your feelings, you are typical of most adults who need to improve their listening and note-taking skills.

Strategy 1   *Determine What You Want from a Lecture or Meeting*

To feel you have gained something from a lecture or meeting, you need to leave that session with a result. You want to have some answers to questions that are important to you.

But how do you motivate yourself to stay focused during the lecture or meeting? As you sit there, a zillion other concerns, projects, or problems zip through your brain. You may have to keep reminding yourself to "Get something out of this session!"

The key to your success as a listener is to carry on a mental dialog with the speaker. As you listen to the speaker, you want to be saying to yourself such things as:

• So that's the point you're making! Yes, I agree with that.

• You don't really believe that, do you? What proof do you have of that?

• That's exactly what I would have said. I'll remember that!

• I don't see what you're getting at. Give me some examples.

There's no end to the comments you can make. The main thing is to direct your effort at agreeing or disagreeing with the speaker. You want to be asking questions about what point the speaker is making and mentally manipulating the information being presented to you.

You will soon recognize that carrying on a mental dialog with the speaker keeps you alert. When you ask questions and mentally argue with a speaker, you get emotionally involved. Your emotionality not only keeps you awake, it makes the speaker's points come alive. The things we remember best are things that are connected with a specific emotion—anger, happiness, disgust, elation, sadness, excitement, whatever.

Sometimes you will get so excited that you will ask a speaker a question. You may ask her to restate what she has said. You may paraphrase back to her what she has said. You may turn to a friend and say, "Is she saying that?" By maintaining your mental and sometimes verbal interaction with the speaker, you'll keep yourself focused on getting answers to your questions.

Strategy 2 — *Keep Track of What Is Said*

It's one thing to keep yourself interested and interacting mentally with the speaker. It's another thing to take notes that make sense and are of use to you. There are keys to successful note taking. Whether you are in a lecture or a business meeting or watching a televised course, the note-taking and listening strategies are identical.

There is one problem we hear time and again from adult learners. They have varying degrees of certainty as to how the information presented in a session will be of use to them. The answer is fairly predictable. What it all boils down to is that your instructor will expect you to be able to answer questions or perform some series of tasks after you have listened to information in a session.

If you buy this concept, it makes sense to write down information for two purposes. You will either rework the information into questions and answers on which you will be tested, or rework the information into a series of instructions that will help you perform specific tasks, such as operate a computer, give a speech, or dissect a frog.

Strategy 3 — *Develop Outlines to Record Information*

How should you record information? What's the best format? To organize information in a way that makes sense to you, the best strategy usually is to put it in outline form.

An outline is simply a logical format for organizing information. The outline form allows you to organize information that you can quickly turn into questions and answers. If you are going to be held responsible for applying the information or if you must answer test questions about it, the outline puts you in a position to see a series of steps you must follow, just as though you were writing a computer program. Whatever the information will be used for, the critical advantage of the outline is that it helps you organize information into logical units that are meaningful.

As with most things, there is no one best strategy for all people. We rely on the thousands of students we have worked with to tell us what works best for them. Most agree with the procedures we have suggested for listening and note taking. The following statements reflect their best advice:

- I don't try to write down everything I hear.

- As I record information, I think about writing down answers to questions.

- I listen for questions the instructor is trying to answer, write them down, listen for the information that answers the questions, and record whatever information might be part of the answer.

- I try to arrange information in some logical order so that I can manipulate the information into questions and answers after the lecture.

- I focus on getting the big picture outlined and rely upon other sources of information to fill in the details I may miss.

- After the lecture or meeting, I go over my outline. If I am going to be tested on the material, I turn the outline into questions and answers.

Strategy 4   *Refine Your Material and Integrate It with Other Information*

There is one procedure that most adults in college agree makes sense. Take your notes on the right-hand page of the notebook and leave the page on the left for developing questions and answers. As soon as possible after the lecture, review your notes to fill in any information you may have left out. This information may come from your friends' notes, readings you are doing in connection with the lecture, or information you pick up in a study group.

The left-hand page is used to restructure the information into the same format on which you will be tested. You say to yourself, "If I were the instructor, what are several questions I would ask on the next exam that come from this page of notes?"

You then write out a few big picture questions. Next, you write a brief answer to each question. You will often find that you have asked good questions that the lecture does not completely answer. Your instructor expects you to go to other sources, such as your text, to develop complete answers.

If you have already completed the reading related to your notes, you will know where to go for the information necessary to complete your answers. If not, you can use your notes to focus your readings. When you read your texts, journal articles, and other sources of information, you'll know what information to look for. It's a fair assumption that the questions instructors allude to in their lectures are the questions they most want students to answer.

Essentially, the left-hand page is the space you will use to integrate information from all sources as you develop the final product of your studies, your questions and answers.

If you are not sure this is the way to go, ask yourself: Have you ever taken a test that didn't ask you to answer questions? You know the answer. So why waste time taking masses of notes that you try to memorize? That's what many adult students do and it doesn't make sense. It just robs you of your time. To win at the learning game, you want to get comfortable looking at the world in terms of questions and answers. And that is what listening and note taking is all about!

Strategy 5 *Use the ADULT Method to Develop Useful Notes*

If Strategies 1–4 make sense to you, then try applying the ADULT method of reading to note taking in the exercise that follows. As you use the ADULT method, try to analyze the notes we took on several pages of a psychology text, *Introduction to Psychology*, by James W. Kalat. These notes cover the material on several pages that focuses on developmental psychology. The actual pages on which the notes were taken are reproduced in Appendix 3 (pp. 177–180). Read those pages before you proceed with the note-taking exercise.

The ADULT method asks you to follow five steps as you analyze your notes:

Ask questions about the information in your notes

Determine and document where your questions are answered in your notes

Understand the information in your notes by reworking it into answers that make sense

Learn the answers by reciting and writing the answers

Test yourself on the questions and answers you developed

As you will see, the ADULT method of note taking is a strategy for making information meaningful and useful. What could be more useful than answers to important questions, some of which will appear on your tests?

Exercise *Apply the ADULT Method of Note Taking*

Ask questions. As you look at the notes we have taken on the material you read, notice that the first thing we have done is to *ask the questions* you will see on the left-hand page of the notes.

Determine where the questions are answered. Your first task is to label in the notes the meaningful information you think supplies the answers to the questions on the left-hand page.

Understand and learn the information. Now take the information you have labeled and rework it into meaningful answers for questions 1–6 on the left-hand page. Writing the answers out is critical to learning them, so write out the answers on the left-hand page.

Test yourself. Test yourself on these questions and answers as if you were preparing for a test on the notes. Look at each question and then talk out an answer. Then go back and compare your answer with the one you wrote earlier to see how well your memory is working.

1. How does Piaget define *schema* and how do the processes of assimilation and accommodation interact with schema?

    ....

    ....

    ....

    ....

    ....

2. List and briefly define Piaget's stages of intellectual development.

    ....

    ....

    ....

    ....

    ....

3. Describe the characteristics of the sensorimotor stage.

    ....

    ....

    ....

    ....

4. Describe the characteristics of the preoperational stage.

    ....

    ....

    ....

    ....

5. Describe the characteristics of the stage of concrete operations.

    ....

    ....

    ....

    ....

    ....

6. Describe the characteristics of the stage of formal operations.

    ....

    ....

    ....

    ....

I. Schema

    A. Mental process through which people interact with objects in an organized way.

        1. Change or adapt schema through assimilation and accommodation.

        2. Processes through which intellectual growth occurs.

    B. Assimilation

        1. Apply an old schema to new objects.

            a. Grasp a new object as you grasp a familiar object.

    C. Accommodation

        1. Modify an old schema to fit a new object.

            a. Infant sucks new objects in different ways to accommodate larger size.

II. Four stages of intellectual development

    A. Sensorimotor stage (birth–$1^{1}/_{2}$ yrs. approx.)

        1. Behavior focuses on simple motor responses.

        2. Infant focuses on what is present, not on what is imagined or remembered.

        3. Infants not capable of representational thought.

            a. Don't think about what they don't see, hear, smell, feel, or sense.

        4. Lack sense of object permanence.

            a. Don't see it, it doesn't exist.

    B. Preoperational stage ($1^{1}/_{2}$–7 yrs. approx.)

        1. Language acquisition dramatic.

            a. Learn nine new words daily.

        2. Acquire concept of object permanence.

        3. Child lacks operations-reversible mental processes.

            a. His brother has no brother.

        4. Accept experiences at face value.

            a. White ball behind blue paper is blue.

        5. Lack conservation.

            a. Objects conserve properties even if shape or arrangement changes.

            b. Can't perform mental operations to make transformations.

            c. When an equal number of objects (such as pennies) are spread out in two rows, the row that appears longer is said to contain more objects.

    C. Stage of concrete operations (7–11 yrs. approx.)

        1. Begin to understand conservation of physical properties.

            a. Squashing a ball doesn't change its weight.

            b. Children perform mental operations on concrete objects.

            c. Children have trouble with abstract or hypothetical ideas.

    D. Stage of formal operations (adolescence–adulthood)

        1. People can now deal with abstract and hypothetical situations.

            a. Logic, deductive reasoning, and planning.

CHAPTER 12

Three Strategies for Preparing to Take Tests

Strategy 1: **Study as though you were preparing to take a test**

Strategy 2: **Gather and practice answering test questions**

Strategy 3: **Practice, practice, practice**

If there's one thing many adult learners fear, it's taking tests. If preparing for and taking tests makes you uncomfortable, you're not alone. With which of the following statements do you agree? With which do you disagree?

Agree   **Disagree**

❏   ❏   I can reduce my fear of tests by always studying as though I were practicing to take a test.

❏   ❏   It would help me to work with other students to develop possible test questions and answers.

❏   ❏   I should spend a lot of time developing possible test questions and answers from my notes and readings.

❏   ❏   It would be helpful to look at old tests to see what my test might look like.

❏   ❏   I should talk with my instructor to find out if my perception of the test is the same as his or hers.

❏   ❏   The course syllabus is a key source of information about possible test questions.

❏   ❏   In class I should ask the questions I think might be on exams.

❏   ❏   With consistent practice, I will become an excellent test taker.

These statements reflect some of the best approaches you can take to prepare for a test. Preparing for and taking tests is one of the most stressful aspects of the academic and professional lives of most adult learners. But it needn't be a problem for you. You can make test preparation and test taking reasonably stress-free. The key is to follow this principle:

Strategy 1   Study as Though You Were Preparing to Take a Test

When you look at what is being asked of you in 99 percent of the tests you take in college or at work, you discover that you are asked to answer questions. It makes sense, then, that your preparation for a test should focus on asking and answering the questions you will later find on your exam.

You have practiced the reading, listening, and note-taking procedures that will position you to prepare for a test. Now you want to look at how to pull all of your questions and answers together as you face an exam.

Your test-preparation plan includes three essential stages. First, you gather all relevant learning materials together and organize them. Then, you develop potential test questions from these materials. Finally, you practice answering those questions.

Strategy 2   Gather and Practice Answering Test Questions

Ask yourself: What are all the possible sources of the test questions and answers? If you have been developing questions and answers from your readings and notes, you may feel that you have an adequate stock of questions and answers with which to prepare.

Go one step further. There are several other sources of questions that can dramatically enhance your performance: fellow students, old tests, ancillary materials, the class syllabus, and questions you can ask in class.

Tactic 1   Use your fellow students as a source of questions and answers:
Think of any job you have ever held. Have you had an opportunity to see how a small group of people can attack a large task and finish it in no time at all? When a group focuses on finding the answers to questions posed by a project, your work load can be dramatically decreased.

The same is true of the tests you face in college. A small group of fellow students can decrease the amount of time you spend scanning various sources for possible test questions and answers. You will also gather insights and improve your understanding of the possible answers. Another person's perspective may help raise a B answer to an A answer.

With your heavy work load, you can't afford to pass up the opportunity to work with colleagues. Your support group may consist of only three people. That's three people who can help you identify questions and develop answers. Members often help one another understand important concepts and procedures that are not fully developed in the readings or by the instructor.

Tactic 2

Use old tests as a guide to your test: Adult learners are often in a quandary when we suggest that they seek out old tests to guide their studying and test preparation. "How can I possibly get my hands on old tests?" This is a special problem for the commuter student who is racing to and from home or a job and campus.

Students have consistently told us that they find instructors far more willing to supply copies of old tests than they would have imagined. Tact and diplomacy appear to be the key. The strategy goes something like this:

You approach your instructor and indicate you need a few seconds of time for guidance. You let your instructor know from the beginning that you have been working hard. You do so by showing him or her the questions and answers you have been developing from the readings and notes for your practice exams.

Your instructor will see that you are a serious student. You are now in a position to ask for your instructor's assistance. The image you have created is that of an anxious, hard-working adult learner.

You can ask your instructor to look over some of your questions. You want to know, "Am I focusing on the issues you think are important?" After your instructor looks over your questions, you can ask for additional assistance.

"Would it be possible to look at some old tests? I'd like to practice taking some old tests. I think then I might not feel so anxious. I tend to panic during exams." Most instructors know that adult learners are anxious about tests and are willing to help you.

The worst thing that can happen is that your instructor will decline the request. Instructors may not have old exams covering the topic or may wish to reuse portions of old tests. Whatever your instructor's response, your questioning will have three important consequences. Your instructor will have given you some idea of the value of the questions you have developed. If your instructor suggests some alternative questions or that you redirect your focus, you have gained valuable information. Of great significance is that you have shown your instructor you are a serious learner. You will find that instructors will be more favorably disposed toward your future work when you have let them see how hard you are working in their class.

You may think it's unlikely that an instructor will supply you with old tests. It's worth asking for them, because you may get the instructor thinking in another direction that will be to your advantage. The instructor may offer an additional review session as an alternative or provide you with a study guide or study sheet. It's not uncommon for faculty to develop a review sheet of topics or questions to cover. But sometimes you have to ask.

What do old tests do for you? Old tests answer several questions:

- What might my test look like?

- How similar are the questions I am developing to the questions my instructor has focused on?

- Does the material I'm studying appear to be the same as the material the old test questions are based on?

- Are the instructor's questions general or specific?

- Do the questions ask me to pull together several areas of the course material or do they focus on small units?

- Do the questions ask me to apply what I know or simply to repeat it?

Tactic 3   ***Use ancillary materials as sources of test questions:*** Your ancillary materials can save you hundreds of hours of work. They include workbooks, study guides, training manuals, and handbooks. These materials often accompany the texts used in college courses and business training programs. Many instructors produce their own ancillary materials to show students what and how they want them to study.

Ancillary materials are loaded with practice questions and answers, yet adult learners often overlook them, perhaps because the instructor fails to mention them. Some instructors use the test questions provided in ancillary materials—a sensible procedure, because these materials are professionally prepared and contain excellent questions. Many instructors save a lot of time by using these questions instead of developing their own.

If you check your college bookstore, you can find out whether an ancillary book is available to accompany your text. The time you will save and the improved scores you will earn on your exams are well worth the expense.

Tactic 4   ***Don't forget to consult your class syllabus:*** Your class syllabus will typically describe the content areas, the key issues on which your course will focus, and related course information.

Sharp students scan the syllabus to gain a feel for the important issues on which the course will focus. These students gear their note taking in class and on readings to the issues and questions presented in the syllabus. Often the syllabus is an excellent source for determining what the essay questions on your exams may look like.

Tactic 5   ***Asking questions in class:*** You want to ask questions you think may be on the exam. An instructor who assigns a journal article or chapter to be read for class is telling you, "I may test you on these readings."

If you read this information with the idea of developing questions your instructor may answer in class, you'll be at a distinct advantage. You will then attend class well prepared to listen for the answers to those questions.

Most instructors appreciate well-focused questions that show that students have read the assigned material. If you ask a question to which your instructor devotes significant time, watch for it on the test.

The Final Keys to Test Preparation Success

With which of the following statements do you now agree? With which do you disagree?

Agree	Disagree	
❏	❏	I should practice quizzing myself on the questions I've developed from all sources of information.
❏	❏	I should talk out the answers to my questions.
❏	❏	I should give myself written quizzes.

Agree   Disagree

❑   ❑   I should work with friends to develop good answers to questions.

❑   ❑   I should have friends or family quiz me on the practice questions.

❑   ❑   I should use old exams to quiz myself.

❑   ❑   I should use questions from study guides to quiz myself.

If you agree with the preceding statements, then your thinking closely matches that of most successful test takers.

Strategy 3   *Practice, Practice, Practice*

You've probably heard the old story about the newcomer to New York who stopped a man carrying a violin case and asked, "Can you tell me how to get to Carnegie Hall?" The man replied: "Practice, practice, practice!"

The critical feature of your test preparation will be your consistent practicing of the behaviors asked of you when you take a test. We have found that the following steps are those that make adult learners most comfortable and competent.

Step 1. Consolidate all of your questions and choose those you feel are most likely to appear on the test. You will have many more questions than your instructor can possibly test you on.

The key is to practice writing as thorough an answer as possible to your high-priority questions. You want to become comfortable producing written answers to questions.

Step 2. Plan to spend several hours writing out answers to questions you think are likely to be on your exam.

Many adult learners say, "But I'm going to have a multiple-choice exam. Why should I write out answers to questions?"

That's a good question. But the fact is that the format of the question is not relevant. Experience has shown that the best way to prepare for any test is to assume that the test will follow an essay format, even if you know otherwise. When you master the answers to your short essay questions, you are prepared to answer the test questions whether they are presented in an essay, multiple-choice, or true-false format.

When people ask you questions, those questions typically call for short answers. You'll seldom be asked, "Which would you choose, A, B, C, or D?" So you needn't worry about what your real test will look like. We just want you to get comfortable answering the questions you feel are important.

Step 3. You may not be able to practice answering all your questions at one sitting. That's fine. You may find that you never have time to answer all your questions completely. That's something you can live with.

You're never going to predict all of your test questions. The important thing is that you are practicing the exact behavior that will be expected of you. As you move through your questions and answers, you will gain confidence in your comprehension of the material. You will feel that you are preparing to do exactly what will be required of you in the test situation. That should give you an added sense of confidence.

As you answer your questions, you may be tempted to look at your notes and texts for confirmation that you are answering the questions correctly. Seeking confirmation is an important strategy. But you will be better off if you answer your questions completely before you confirm your answer or see that you need to make a change.

Adult learners tell us that after they answer all of their questions the first time through, they often get anxious because they realize that they don't remember the material verbatim. If you feel this way, don't worry. Practicing for tests is just like practicing for a speech. The first time through, your speech is rough. As you answer your questions, don't panic if you can't adequately answer questions on specific topics. Simply take the time to go back and review the materials on that topic. Then try the questions again. After a couple of practice runs, you will smooth out the rough spots and feel ready to step to the podium. In other words, if you practice beforehand, when the time comes to take the test, all the cues will be there and you will do very well.

CHAPTER 13

Ten Strategies for Taking Tests

Strategy 1: Read directions carefully

Strategy 2: Survey the test

Strategy 3: Flow with the information you know

Strategy 4: Review test answers

Strategy 5: Demonstrate organization in your essay answers

Strategy 6: Define the terms you use

Strategy 7: Let examples make your points

Strategy 8: Formulate conclusions that integrate the major points

Strategy 9: Examine all options

Strategy 10: Practice for tests by taking practice tests

Adult students often jump into a test without a well-thought-out plan. They just start with the first question and move on. You can develop a better strategy. With which of the following statements do you agree? With which do you disagree?

Agree Disagree

❏ ❏   My first step in taking a test should be to survey the test to see how it should be approached.

❏ ❏   I should skip any questions I'm not sure of and go back to them later.

❏ ❏   When answering multiple-choice questions, I should first eliminate incorrect options.

❏ ❏   I should feel free to change my original answer to a question if I feel confident the change is correct.

❏ ❏   I should develop a format for answering essay questions that earns me the maximum number of points.

❏ ❏   I should save time at the end of the test to make sure I have answered all the questions completely.

    If you agreed with these statements, you're on the right track. Just as you approach reading assignments with the ADULT method we described in Chapter 10, you need to approach tests with procedures that maximize your chance of scoring the most points. The following strategies for test taking will help you become a more efficient and effective test taker.

Strategy 1   *Read Directions Carefully*

Surprisingly, a significant number of people fail to read the directions carefully. These people are anxious to get started. They assume they know how to proceed and just forge ahead. Failing to read the directions carefully may cost you a lot of points.

Strategy 2   *Survey the Test*

Yes   No

❑   ❑   Do you typically look over your test to determine the format and how the test should be attacked?

If you do, take a few seconds now to review the way you survey your tests. Do you typically ask the following questions as you survey?

Yes   No

❑   ❑   What types of questions are being asked on the test?

❑   ❑   What is the point value of the questions?

❑   ❑   With which questions should I start?

❑   ❑   Will answering the first set of questions help me do better on another set of questions?

❑   ❑   Are the questions similar to what I thought I would see?

❑   ❑   How should I divide my time to be sure I allow enough time for each portion of the test?

❑   ❑   Are there easy sets of questions I can complete rapidly to build my confidence for tougher sections?

By quickly surveying or scanning the test, you will be better prepared to complete the test in the time allowed.

Strategy 3   *Flow with the Information You Know*

After a quick survey, you should now be ready to start answering your questions. You want to move rapidly. When you come to questions that stump you, place a mark by them and move on to the next question. Wasting time on a few difficult questions and then being forced to complete other questions under time pressure is unnecessary. On the other hand, noting the challenging questions increases the likelihood that you will think of the answer while you're answering other questions.

Once you have completed the test, you can go back to unanswered questions. What you are trying to do is maintain a positive outlook. You let your brain mull over the questions that stump you as you move on to answer easier questions. Our experience in test taking has shown us that you are less likely to freeze on tests if you keep completing the more obvious questions. You don't want to waste time on questions that baffle you.

Scientists are unsure what is going on in your brain as you skip difficult questions and attack easier ones. Some scientists hypothesize that as you answer easier questions, your brain is analyzing the various possibilities of the more difficult questions. Your brain is trying to integrate new information you have come across in the test. Your brain will then go back and make a more educated approach to the questions you skipped.

Regardless of what is going on in your brain, this procedure will keep you cool and allow you to maintain a sense of confidence as you progress in your test.

Strategy 4   *Review Test Answers*

Once you have completed your test, you will want to take a few minutes to scan it to make sure you have completed each section. Take a few minutes to review questions about which you had some uncertainty and to proofread all written parts of the exam.

If you've been told it's usually unwise to change your original answer, don't believe it. The myth that your first answer is usually the right answer is just that—a myth. Research has shown that if you are well prepared for the test, it may be to your advantage to change some answers.

Suppose you suddenly feel that you ought to change your answer to a multiple-choice question that you weren't quite certain about earlier. As you went through the entire test, you may have exposed yourself to clues that have helped you refocus your thinking. If you feel strongly that you should change your answer, don't hesitate.

Now that we have talked about the basic steps to test taking, we need to go one step further. Let's look at some procedures that are specifically relevant to what have become the two most common forms of exams given in higher education: the essay exam and the multiple-choice exam.

Mastering Essay Tests

What is it that most instructors want to see in a good essay answer? When you ask instructors, they often say things like "I want to see that students can think." What they mean is that students' answers should demonstrate that they have read and understood the material that answers the questions.

Students should be able to integrate what they have read with what they have heard in lectures and formulate thorough answers that make sense. That seems fair enough. But what do thorough answers that make sense look like? By comparing hundreds of answers to essay questions, we have developed a model of the characteristics that are typically found in answers that have received a B or an A.

Strategy 5   *Demonstrate Organization in Your Essay Answers*

If your answer is well organized, it sends a clear message to your instructor: This student has spent some time thinking about this question. To show how well organized your thoughts are, you may wish to develop a short outline of the major points you will address in your answer. A short outline preceding your answer testifies to your organizational skills. And if you run out of time before you complete the essay, the instructor may give you at least partial credit on the basis of the outline.

Your outline will also help you focus your thoughts and maintain your focus as you write your answer. The problem that many students face is that they don't know when to stop writing. Your outline tells you what to say and what *not* to say.

You will want to start your answer with the introduction that tells the reader the intent of your answer. By telling the reader the points you intend to make or the questions you intend to answer, you provide your reader with a focus.

The body of your answer should be composed of paragraphs that build upon one another. Your paragraphs will present in a logical order the points you want to make. If you work from an outline, you simply follow your outline, building your case.

If you use subheadings as you write, you will find that the order of what you are saying is more apparent to the reader. You will also find that your subheadings are used by the grader to assign points.

Strategy 6   *Define the Terms You Use*

As you develop your answer, it is important that you *always* define technical terms. By clarifying terms, you will tell the reader exactly how you interpret information. The reader will analyze your definition and say, "Oh, that's how she sees it. Now I know where she's going." You want to leave no uncertainty in the reader's mind.

Strategy 7   *Let Examples Make Your Points*

All good answers are based on facts. When you give examples that substantiate your points, you leave little room for doubt. The more experts you can quote, studies you can cite, and illustrations you can give, the more points you will earn. A reader who is given several good examples is likely to think, "This student has really given some thought to this issue. She has read the material."

Strategy 8   ***Formulate Conclusions That***
Quickly Integrate the Major Points

Let your conclusion be short and to the point. *End with strength*. Too often students feel they have to summarize their entire paper in the conclusion. After all is said and done, you need not say it again. Simply use the most important key words in a quick summary and be done with it.

Mastering Objective Tests

Hundreds of books have been written on how to take objective tests. Each book is loaded with tons of sample questions and tips on how to go about analyzing the various options in multiple-choice questions.

You won't hurt yourself by reading these books, but your time will be better spent practicing answering questions. This is why we strongly recommend reviewing old tests, developing practice tests, using ancillary materials with practice questions, and encouraging your instructors to supply review sheets.

As we emphasized in Strategy 1, *always read directions*. This is especially critical on objective tests, because several variations are used in the presentation of such questions.

When you get to the test and face those multiple-choice questions, there are several procedures that will earn you points. As you read the directions, watch to see whether you will lose points for answering questions incorrectly. From time to time an instructor will subtract points for incorrect answers. Few instructors follow this procedure, but don't take it for granted that yours won't.

Strategy 9   ***Examine All Options***

When you attack multiple-choice questions, you may find them easier to answer if you follow these steps:

1. Read the question and all the options. Eliminate the absolutely incorrect answers. If only one remains, you're in good shape.

2. If, after you have eliminated options, two or more are still available, two procedures may help you.

   a. Read the question and try to develop an answer. Then look at the remaining options and see if one option is now a more obvious answer.

   b. If you are still unsure, read the question again and combine it with each option separately to see if one of them is a logical fit.

3. Remember that *"All of the above" and "None of the above" are seldom correct*. When a multiple-choice question includes one of these options, be cautious. If the option is "None of the above," you have to make sure that something is wrong with each of the other options. If it's "All of

the above," none of the other options can be incorrect. We mention these two options because we are surprised how often instructors tempt students with them and how often students fall for them.

The experts give hundreds of little tips on test taking. The tips we have offered are those our students have told us are most useful. But, according to our students over the past 25 years, the *best tip we ever gave them is*:

Strategy 10   *Practice for Tests by Taking Practice Tests*

There's no need to panic. Over the past 20 years, hundreds of psychological studies have been performed on how to reduce exam anxiety. Deep breathing, desensitization, meditation, and visualizing a successful test are among the procedures that have been used with varying degrees of success. Students who use these procedures gain confidence in their ability to perform and are often more relaxed when the time comes to take the test. But their test results seldom change dramatically.

Although these techniques can teach students to learn to relax, they have typically failed to teach students how to prepare for exams. The key to doing well in any area of performance is to practice the behavior you will have to perform.

Visualizing that you will knock this test on its backside is great. What will make you feel even greater is knowing that you have practiced developing and answering the questions you are about to face.

Is This the Magic Solution to My Test-Taking Fears?

You often hear experts, whether they are tennis pros, directors of weight loss programs, or world-class pianists, hedge their advice by saying, "No one approach is best for anyone." We take a somewhat different position in regard to taking tests.

We encourage you to look at your style and adapt it to accord with the advice we have just given you. We are not the least hesitant to say that what we have just told you is good for everyone. Whatever test-taking skills you already have will be dramatically enhanced if you alter your approach to include the ten strategies we have put at your fingertips.

In the course of this book we have described more than 40 strategies that will help you achieve your academic, personal, and professional goals. These approaches focus on ways to manage your time and yourself and ways to enhance your ability to learn. All of these skills are important components of success, interrelating and reinforcing each other. The opportunity to apply specific learning skills, for example, often depends on effective time management, and your attitudes toward yourself as a learner affect your capacity to plan for success. These skills have been discussed as discrete strategies, but in reality they are inseparable, working together to define your progress toward your goals.

All of the strategies address issues of change as you grapple with the challenges you confront. Use these strategies and insights as you continue to create your preferred future. They will serve you well, providing the framework for your success now and in the future. We indicated from the outset that this book would be about change. Indeed, it has been about change and about the future as well—the one you will create for yourself.

APPENDIX 1

Personal Action Plan

Filled-in Personal Action Plans are provided in this appendix to demonstrate how two adult learners developed their plans. They are intended only to serve as a guide. Be creative in your own approach to developing *your* Personal Action Plan. Involve others in helping you to think through your own situation and to complete the action steps.

Until you have used the Personal Action Plan process a few times, we suggest that you read the instructions in Chapter 2 as you proceed through the action steps. Three blank sets of forms are provided here for your use.

The first set of filled-in Personal Action Plans belongs to Sharon, an adult learner, 33-years-old, who returned to school part-time to earn her bachelor's degree in preparation to become an elementary school teacher. This term she is taking three courses to meet her basic distribution requirements.

Her husband is a factory worker with an inflexible work schedule; she has three young children aged 6, 10, and 13, all of whom are (at last) now in school. She formerly worked in sales and as a secretary. She has a computer and laser printer in her home and does word processing on a freelance basis.

She was fairly apprehensive about going back to school, but she belongs to an adult-learner support group and has found the time-management material and these forms to be very helpful.

The second set of filled-in Personal Action Plans was developed by Bruce, 27-years-old, who started working at a small electronics company upon high school graduation.

As the company grew so did Bruce's opportunities. Two years ago he was promoted to a salaried position and began working as an accounting clerk in the business office. Further promotion is blocked unless he obtains an accounting degree. His employer has initiated a tuition reimbursement program and is encouraging Bruce to get his degree as soon as possible.

Bruce's wife, a college graduate, works full-time; they have a three-year-old daughter, day care expenses, and some anxiety over what Bruce's going to college will do to their quality of life.

Bruce is concerned also that he won't be able to compete with younger students or might not be able to do college work, even though he shows outstanding aptitude at work. He will not be the first in his family to attend college, but he will be the first to graduate.

Sharon's Personal Action Plan

Date *September, 19XX*

Action Step 1

Develop your change scenario: A change scenario is a short essay about yourself similar to the comments you have read earlier. Write about what's happening in your life that is creating an interest in or a need to change. In other words, describe your opportunities for change.

> I always promised myself that when my youngest child entered elementary school, I would go to college and get a teaching degree. My youngest is six now and in school. And I still want to teach. I've worked as a secretary and as a salesperson before I got married, but I am scared about going to college.

Action Step 2

Describe your vision for change—your preferred future: What will happen to you as a result of the change you envision? When you write, imagine that the change has already taken place and describe what you or your situation look like as though it had already happened. Write, therefore, in the present tense. Describe how things look, how they differ from the way they used to be. And don't forget to indicate what month and year this is so that you will know how long you have given yourself to implement your vision for change.

> I'm a first-grade teacher and I love it. I especially like teaching children to read. At the end of each day I feel I've made a real difference in their lives — a contribution. My own children and husband treat me with greater respect. We all welcome the income.

Action Step 3   *Translate your vision into goal statements:* List your goals in the accompanying table and indicate whether they are for the short term (one to two years), the intermediate term (three to four years), or the long term (five or more years). Then restate those goals to indicate what they will look like when you've achieved them.

Goal number	Goal statement	How it will look when achieved	Time frame (years) 1–2	3–4	5+
1.	Work out a household routine so I'll have time for classes & study and continue to do all I presently have to do.	I'll be able to go to classes & find enough study time, working around a schedule that includes: • 16 hrs per week free-lance word processing in my home • driving the kids to their lessons/doctors • time w/my husband (bowling league & our Sat. nite out together) • household chores • being home when the kids are out of school	✓		
2.	Go to school at least ½ time, prefer ¾ time, each semester until I graduate w/a teaching degree.	I will go to school Fall, Winter & Spring terms, taking 2-3 classes each term. I'll take certification requirements in more than 1 subject to help me get a job when I graduate.		✓	
3.	Get a teaching job with decent pay and full benefits.	I'll teach in an elementary school w/a work day that has similar hours to those of my own kids at their schools. I'll have specialties in reading & either science or language arts to help me get & maintain my job. I will earn a respectable salary & receive full benefits			✓

Action Step 4   *List in the accompanying table all positive or facilitating forces you can think of that will help you achieve each goal you have listed:* Forces can be *within yourself* (I want to earn more money; I want to be promoted) or *within your family* (my children are grown up and out of the house; we need extra income to pay for our children's college) or *within your work or learning environment* (I have a new boss who demands that I get a college degree; I want to be able to compete with new employees who are better educated than I am). As you develop this analysis you will find that some forces are moving you toward more than one goal. It's not necessary to list a force more than once; just note all the goals each force facilitates.

Action Step 5   *List in the accompanying table all negative or blocking forces that will impede your progress toward each goal you have identified:* Again, it's not necessary to repeat any force that is blocking your progress toward more than one goal; just note all the goals each force is blocking. Some blocking forces we've heard about: "I'm frightened about the change." "I didn't go to school originally because I wasn't sure I would be successful." "My husband and children say they need me at home full-time." "My boss expects me to go to school, but my co-workers expect me to produce just as much and participate in extra overload assignments."

List all positive or facilitating forces	List all negative or blocking forces
Inside yourself I really want these: • a college degree • to teach • more income for the family I'm creative and good with kids. I'm a good mom, so I'm experienced — in a sense.	Scared - afraid of failing & of not knowing what to do Unsure around educated people Intimidated by the young college kids * I'll need a lot of time to study — I'm out of practice!
Within your family and other relationships My husband wants me to do this because he knows I always wanted to. * my mom can help w/ the kids * my neighbors will help me My kids are cooperative & helpful.	* My husband has no time flexibility w/ his job to help take care of the kids or w/ household chores * my husband is a little afraid it will hurt our relationship * Cost!
Within your work or learning environment School is nearby. * I have friends who are returning students there	* classes I need are hard to schedule in blocks (time) when my kids are in school * will require me to have a car

Action Step 6   **Review Action Steps 4 and 5 and mark with an asterisk(*) the facilitating and blocking forces you can do something about immediately:** Focus on these forces first. As time goes on you can work on the others, but it's important to have a starting point. It's best to start with what can be changed *now*.

Action Step 7   **Mobilize for change:** Review the forces you marked with an asterisk (*) in Action Steps 4 and 5. Transfer the facilitating forces to the lefthand column of the following table. For each force you have recorded in the lefthand column, list all the ideas, means, and resources you can use to make these forces work more strongly for you.

Action Step 8   **Mobilize for change:** Review the forces you marked with an asterisk (*) in Action Steps 4 and 5. Transfer the blocking forces to the righthand column of the following table. For each force you have recorded in the righthand column, list all the ideas, means, and resources you can use to remove or cope with these forces.

Action Step 7   *Action Step 8*

Facilitating forces	Blocking forces
Force: Friends who have returned to school: a) speak to them about ways they have managed b) meet more adult learners to study together	Force: Cost: a) Investigate financial aid & loans b) Investigate grants for returning adult students
Force: Neighbors & Mom willing to help w/childcare a) speak to them & make concrete plans for regular swaps or payment	Force: Car: a) Buy used car Force: Class times: a) Arrange childcare to cover days when I need to take afternoon classes
Force: Use my experience as a mom to get volunteer or paid work in schools to improve my resume before I graduate	Force: Husband can't help: a) Get more organized & get kids to do some chores b) Eliminate some chores Force: Husband afraid will hurt our relationship a) Speak to him about his feelings

Action Step 9   ***Determine major change tactics:*** Review all of the information in Action Steps 7 and 8 and decide which ones are critical for achieving your goals. Write each of your change tactics in the accompanying table.

Action Step 10   ***Create a comprehensive action plan:*** Number the square in front of each change tactic to indicate the order in which these steps should be taken. After you have completed Action Steps 9 and 10, we suggest you rewrite your action plan in priority order, following the format of the accompanying table.

	Change tactics	Members of my change team who should be involved	Other resources available	Anticipated completion date
2	Get more organized at home	The Family	Campus sessions on Time Mng.	First year
5	Get car	Husband		2 months
4	Get childcare coverage	Husband, Mom, neighbors		1 month
3	Speak to Financial Aid	Financial Aid Office	Books & grant info.	3 weeks
6	Eliminate activities that divert me from my goal	Speak to friends & explain my change		First year
1	Speak to kids & husband about change	Husband & kids	a) Counselor on campus b) Program Coordinator of Adult Learners	NOW

Action Step 11   *Describe what early progress will look like for each change tactic:* State each step in clear and concise terms that are oriented toward your end results.

Action Step 12   *Keep things moving forward:* Identify what needs to be done to keep things progressing toward your goals.

	Action Step 11	**Action Step 12**
Change tactic number	**Progress description**	**What needs to be done to move ahead**
1.	Spoke to husband & each child alone & then together. We listed their ideas & fears & talked about them.	Try their ideas systematically. Exp: Teach them to make their own lunches & make their own beds.
2.	Get more organized. Keep time management sheets to see where time goes.	Make better use of waiting time on campus, at kids' activities, and in the evenings.
3.	Appt. at Financial Aid – get forms	Fill out forms & apply. Need references too.
4.	Arranged child care	Get family & friends to help cover for me when my schedule conflicts with children's schedule
5.	To get car – follow ads	Follow up on car ads.
6.	Eliminate some T.V. watching & volunteer work	Still need to spend less time on phone!

Action Step 13   *Review and revise your plan each week or as appropriate:* This is a crucial step. As you proceed through school and face the challenges that lie ahead in your life, circumstances will change. There will be new goals and new forces that will help and hinder you, but you will be equipped with a powerful way to analyze the situation and to develop successful strategies to achieve your goals.

Bruce's Personal Action Plan

Date   Sept. 1

Action Step 1   ***Develop your change scenario:*** A change scenario is a short essay about yourself similar to the comments you have read earlier. Write about what's happening in your life that is creating an interest in or a need to change. In other words, describe your opportunities for change.

> I know that I can make a better career for myself than I have now. I know I want to be an accountant and with the support of my employer and my wife, I know that I can accomplish this goal. It will be difficult in the next several years to manage work, home, and school, but I have made my mind up that this is something I need and want to do. I know that this degree is an important part of making a better future for myself and my family.

Action Step 2   ***Describe your vision for change—your preferred future:*** What will happen to you as a result of the change you envision? When you write, imagine that the change has already taken place and describe what you or your situation look like as though it had already happened. Write, therefore, in the present tense. Describe how things look, how they differ from the way they used to be. And don't forget to indicate what month and year this is so that you will know how long you have given yourself to implement your vision for change.

> It is now five years down the road and I have graduated with a degree in accounting. I soon will be promoted to a professional accounting position in the company where I have been working. The last five years were pretty tough, but by organizing my time well, I was able to keep up with my schedule and still have time for my family. I am more confident about the future because of my degree - things look very bright for me now.

Action Step 3   ***Translate your vision into goal statements:*** List your goals in the accompanying table and indicate whether they are for the short term (one to two years), the intermediate term (three to four years), or the long term (five or more years). Then restate those goals to indicate what they will look like when you've achieved them.

Goal number	Goal statement	How it will look when achieved	Time frame (years) 1–2	3–4	5+
1.	Develop a plan to go to school and work and still have some time for my family.	I will work 30 hrs/wk, take 4 classes per semester, study approx. 20 hrs/wk and schedule time for wife + child.	✓		
2.	Graduate from college within 5 years with a degree in accounting.	I will have been able to keep up with classes, studying, + work while keeping time for my family + myself.		✓	
3.	Will be appointed to a professional accounting position in the electronics company where I currently work.	I will have a new, challenging career with lots of potential for advancement and my family will be more financially secure.			✓

Action Step 4   **List in the accompanying table all positive or facilitating forces you can think of that will help you achieve each goal you have listed:** Forces can be *within yourself* (I want to earn more money; I want to be promoted) or *within your family* (my children are grown up and out of the house; we need extra income to pay for our children's college) or *within your work or learning environment* (I have a new boss who demands that I get a college degree; I want to be able to compete with new employees who are better educated than I am). As you develop this analysis you will find that some forces are moving you toward more than one goal. It's not necessary to list a force more than once; just note all the goals each force facilitates.

Action Step 5   **List in the accompanying table all negative or blocking forces that will impede your progress toward each goal you have identified:** Again, it's not necessary to repeat any force that is blocking your progress toward more than one goal; just note all the goals each force is blocking. Some blocking forces we've heard about: "I'm frightened about the change." "I didn't go to school originally because I wasn't sure I would be successful." "My husband and children say they need me at home full-time." "My boss expects me to go to school, but my co-workers expect me to produce just as much and participate in extra overload assignments."

List all positive or facilitating forces	List all negative or blocking forces
Inside yourself * – I learn quickly + I have a great desire to succeed – It has been a dream of mine to be a college graduate – I want a better future for myself + my family	– I might feel out of place w/ the younger students – I'm used to doing well at work – but college is totally new... I'm not sure what to expect. * – I will be under considerable pressure for a long period of time
Within your family and other relationships * – my wife is very supportive of my going to college. * – we are all able to help each other out w/ tasks at home * – my mom + sister live closely if we need to have child care	– will have less time for wife + daughter * – my wife has a full-time job, so she doesn't have a lot of extra time to spare either * – our family + friends will think I'm neglecting them.
Within your work or learning environment – my boss is very supportive + wants me to get a college degree * – the company will pay for my tuition + fees * – my schedule can be flexible	* – I will be working less hours + there is always a lot of pressure to get more done – my boss + co-workers might feel I am not pulling my load + might be jealous or angry

Action Step 6   ***Review Action Steps 4 and 5 and mark with an asterisk(*) the facilitating and blocking forces you can do something about immediately:*** Focus on these forces first. As time goes on you can work on the others, but it's important to have a starting point. It's best to start with what can be changed *now*.

Action Step 7   ***Mobilize for change:*** Review the forces you marked with an asterisk (*) in Action Steps 4 and 5. Transfer the facilitating forces to the lefthand column of the following table. For each force you have recorded in the lefthand column, list all the ideas, means, and resources you can use to make these forces work more strongly for you.

Action Step 8   ***Mobilize for change:*** Review the forces you marked with an asterisk (*) in Action Steps 4 and 5. Transfer the blocking forces to the righthand column of the following table. For each force you have recorded in the righthand column, list all the ideas, means, and resources you can use to remove or cope with these forces.

Action Step 7   Action Step 8

Facilitating forces	Blocking forces
Force: I learn quickly – find out as much as I can about returning to college – talk to professors, other students to get advice w/classes + studying – follow advice in the Adult Learner's Success book	Force: Under considerable pressure until I get degree – recognize my limits + make sure I don't get into commitments that add to my stress – keep family, friends + people at work up to date about my schedule
Force: Wife + family are supportive – work out my schedule w/ my wife to make sure she understands how I plan to use my time + when I am available – make a list of chores that each of us will be responsible for.	Force: My wife has full-time job + very limited amount of spare time – need to be sensitive to her needs – will have to make sure we have time to spend together – will have to be more flexible about important things
Force: Boss + company are supportive + will pay for school + schedule is flexible. – notify boss of exam and classes + keep fully informed about my progress. If I have extra time, let him know I can help out	Force: Expectations at work to always do more. – need to work hard while I am at work. – if can help out co-workers within time limits try to do so – be very appreciative + show it

Action Step 9   ***Determine major change tactics:*** Review all of the information in Action Steps 7 and 8 and decide which ones are critical for achieving your goals. Write each of your change tactics in the accompanying table.

Action Step 10   ***Create a comprehensive action plan:*** Number the square in front of each change tactic to indicate the order in which these steps should be taken. After you have completed Action Steps 9 and 10, we suggest you rewrite your action plan in priority order, following the format of the accompanying table.

	Change tactics	Members of my change team who should be involved	Other resources available	Anticipated completion date
2	Develop a written plan for my success at school, work + home	Wife, family, boss + co-workers	—	now
1	Make sure I get good class schedule for next term.	Academic advisor	—	now
5	Develop a course plan for now until graduation	Academic advisor	—	This semester
4	Work out schedule for my home responsibilities	Wife	Mother, sister	1 mo.
3	Let work know my schedule for next term	—	—	now
6	Check out resources on campus for adult learners	adult student group, advisor, instructor of orientation course	Student newspaper, friends	1st semester

Action Step 11   ***Describe what early progress will look like for each change tactic:*** State each step in clear and concise terms that are oriented toward your end results.

Action Step 12   ***Keep things moving forward:*** Identify what needs to be done to keep things progressing toward your goals.

Action Step 11   **Action Step 12**

Change tactic number	Progress description	What needs to be done to move ahead
1	Meet w/ academic advisor to schedule next term's courses	– schedule appointment – read catalog to understand requirements
2	I have a written plan for school, work + home	– use the forms in this book to plan my year ahead – discuss my needs w/ academic advisor, boss + wife – get them to help me develop plan so they will feel part of my success
3	Keep work informed of my schedule	– give schedule to my boss – talk w/ boss + co-workers about what duties need to be reassigned
4	Set up schedule w/ my wife for duties at home	– go out to dinner together to discuss our plans
5	Develop long-range academic plan	– find out all requirements – map out courses + when to take them – meet w/ academic advisor + College of Business advisor
6	Find out about special resources for adult learners	– Check out organization for adult learners – read student newspaper – visit different offices on campus between classes

Action Step 13   ***Review and revise your plan each week or as appropriate:*** This is a crucial step. As you proceed through school and face the challenges that lie ahead in your life, circumstances will change. There will be new goals and new forces that will help and hinder you, but you will be equipped with a powerful way to analyze the situation and to develop successful strategies to achieve your goals.

Personal Action Plan

Date
....

Action Step 1   ***Develop your change scenario:*** A change scenario is a short essay about yourself similar to the comments you have read earlier. Write about what's happening in your life that is creating an interest in or a need to change. In other words, describe your opportunities for change.

....
....
....
....
....
....
....
....
....
....

Action Step 2   ***Describe your vision for change—your preferred future:*** What will happen to you as a result of the change you envision? When you write, imagine that the change has already taken place and describe what you or your situation look like as though it had already happened. Write, therefore, in the present tense. Describe how things look, how they differ from the way they used to be. And don't forget to indicate what month and year this is so that you will know how long you have given yourself to implement your vision for change.

....
....
....
....
....
....
....
....
....

Action Step 3   ***Translate your vision into goal statements:*** List your goals in the accompanying table and indicate whether they are for the short term (one to two years), the intermediate term (three to four years), or the long term (five or more years). Then restate those goals to indicate what they will look like when you've achieved them.

Goal number	Goal statement	How it will look when achieved	Time frame (years) 1–2	3–4	5+

Action Step 4   ***List in the accompanying table all positive or facilitating forces you can think of that will help you achieve each goal you have listed:*** Forces can be *within yourself* (I want to earn more money; I want to be promoted) or *within your family* (my children are grown up and out of the house; we need extra income to pay for our children's college) or *within your work or learning environment* (I have a new boss who demands that I get a college degree; I want to be able to compete with new employees who are better educated than I am). As you develop this analysis you will find that some forces are moving you toward more than one goal. It's not necessary to list a force more than once; just note all the goals each force facilitates.

Action Step 5   ***List in the accompanying table all negative or blocking forces that will impede your progress toward each goal you have identified:*** Again, it's not necessary to repeat any force that is blocking your progress toward more than one goal; just note all the goals each force is blocking. Some blocking forces we've heard about: "I'm frightened about the change." "I didn't go to school originally because I wasn't sure I would be successful." "My husband and children say they need me at home full-time." "My boss expects me to go to school, but my co-workers expect me to produce just as much and participate in extra overload assignments."

List all positive or facilitating forces	List all negative or blocking forces
Inside yourself	
Within your family and other relationships	
Within your work or learning environment	

Action Step 6   ***Review Action Steps 4 and 5 and mark with an asterisk(*) the facilitating and blocking forces you can do something about immediately:*** Focus on these forces first. As time goes on you can work on the others, but it's important to have a starting point. It's best to start with what can be changed *now*.

Action Step 7   ***Mobilize for change:*** Review the forces you marked with an asterisk (*) in Action Steps 4 and 5. Transfer the facilitating forces to the lefthand column of the following table. For each force you have recorded in the lefthand column, list all the ideas, means, and resources you can use to make these forces work more strongly for you.

Action Step 8   ***Mobilize for change:*** Review the forces you marked with an asterisk (*) in Action Steps 4 and 5. Transfer the blocking forces to the righthand column of the following table. For each force you have recorded in the righthand column, list all the ideas, means, and resources you can use to remove or cope with these forces.

Action Step 7   *Action Step 8*

Facilitating forces	Blocking forces
Force:	**Force:**
Force:	**Force:**
Force:	**Force:**

Action Step 9   ***Determine major change tactics:*** Review all of the information in Action Steps 7 and 8 and decide which ones are critical for achieving your goals. Write each of your change tactics in the accompanying table.

Action Step 10   ***Create a comprehensive action plan:*** Number the square in front of each change tactic to indicate the order in which these steps should be taken. After you have completed Action Steps 9 and 10, we suggest you rewrite your action plan in priority order, following the format of the accompanying table.

	Change tactics	Members of my change team who should be involved	Other resources available	Anticipated completion date
☐				
☐				
☐				
☐				
☐				
☐				
☐				
☐				
☐				
☐				
☐				

Action Step 11 **Describe what early progress will look like for each change tactic:** State each step in clear and concise terms that are oriented toward your end results.

Action Step 12 **Keep things moving forward:** Identify what needs to be done to keep things progressing toward your goals.

	Action Step 11	**Action Step 12**
Change tactic number	**Progress description**	**What needs to be done to move ahead**

Action Step 13 **Review and revise your plan each week or as appropriate:** This is a crucial step. As you proceed through school and face the challenges that lie ahead in your life, circumstances will change. There will be new goals and new forces that will help and hinder you, but you will be equipped with a powerful way to analyze the situation and to develop successful strategies to achieve your goals.

Personal Action Plan

Date ....

Action Step 1   ***Develop your change scenario:*** A change scenario is a short essay about yourself similar to the comments you have read earlier. Write about what's happening in your life that is creating an interest in or a need to change. In other words, describe your opportunities for change.

....

....

....

....

....

....

....

....

....

Action Step 2   ***Describe your vision for change—your preferred future:*** What will happen to you as a result of the change you envision? When you write, imagine that the change has already taken place and describe what you or your situation look like as though it had already happened. Write, therefore, in the present tense. Describe how things look, how they differ from the way they used to be. And don't forget to indicate what month and year this is so that you will know how long you have given yourself to implement your vision for change.

....

....

....

....

....

....

....

....

....

Action Step 3   ***Translate your vision into goal statements:*** List your goals in the accompanying table and indicate whether they are for the short term (one to two years), the intermediate term (three to four years), or the long term (five or more years). Then restate those goals to indicate what they will look like when you've achieved them.

Goal number	Goal statement	How it will look when achieved	Time frame (years) 1–2	3–4	5+

Action Step 4   ***List in the accompanying table all positive or facilitating forces you can think of that will help you achieve each goal you have listed:*** Forces can be *within yourself* (I want to earn more money; I want to be promoted) or *within your family* (my children are grown up and out of the house; we need extra income to pay for our children's college) or *within your work or learning environment* (I have a new boss who demands that I get a college degree; I want to be able to compete with new employees who are better educated than I am). As you develop this analysis you will find that some forces are moving you toward more than one goal. It's not necessary to list a force more than once; just note all the goals each force facilitates.

Action Step 5   ***List in the accompanying table all negative or blocking forces that will impede your progress toward each goal you have identified:*** Again, it's not necessary to repeat any force that is blocking your progress toward more than one goal; just note all the goals each force is blocking. Some blocking forces we've heard about: "I'm frightened about the change." "I didn't go to school originally because I wasn't sure I would be successful." "My husband and children say they need me at home full-time." "My boss expects me to go to school, but my co-workers expect me to produce just as much and participate in extra overload assignments."

List all positive or facilitating forces	List all negative or blocking forces
Inside yourself	
Within your family and other relationships	
Within your work or learning environment	

Action Step 6 *Review Action Steps 4 and 5 and mark with an asterisk(*) the facilitating and blocking forces you can do something about immediately:* Focus on these forces first. As time goes on you can work on the others, but it's important to have a starting point. It's best to start with what can be changed *now*.

Action Step 7 *Mobilize for change:* Review the forces you marked with an asterisk (*) in Action Steps 4 and 5. Transfer the facilitating forces to the lefthand column of the following table. For each force you have recorded in the lefthand column, list all the ideas, means, and resources you can use to make these forces work more strongly for you.

Action Step 8 *Mobilize for change:* Review the forces you marked with an asterisk (*) in Action Steps 4 and 5. Transfer the blocking forces to the righthand column of the following table. For each force you have recorded in the righthand column, list all the ideas, means, and resources you can use to remove or cope with these forces.

Action Step 7   *Action Step 8*

Facilitating forces	Blocking forces
Force:	Force:
Force:	Force:
Force:	Force:

Action Step 9   ***Determine major change tactics:*** Review all of the information in Action Steps 7 and 8 and decide which ones are critical for achieving your goals. Write each of your change tactics in the accompanying table.

Action Step 10   ***Create a comprehensive action plan:*** Number the square in front of each change tactic to indicate the order in which these steps should be taken. After you have completed Action Steps 9 and 10, we suggest you rewrite your action plan in priority order, following the format of the accompanying table.

	Change tactics	Members of my change team who should be involved	Other resources available	Anticipated completion date
☐				
☐				
☐				
☐				
☐				
☐				
☐				
☐				
☐				
☐				
☐				

Action Step 11   *Describe what early progress will look like for each change tactic:* State each step in clear and concise terms that are oriented toward your end results.

Action Step 12   *Keep things moving forward:* Identify what needs to be done to keep things progressing toward your goals.

	Action Step 11	*Action Step 12*
Change tactic number	**Progress description**	**What needs to be done to move ahead**

Action Step 13   *Review and revise your plan each week or as appropriate:* This is a crucial step. As you proceed through school and face the challenges that lie ahead in your life, circumstances will change. There will be new goals and new forces that will help and hinder you, but you will be equipped with a powerful way to analyze the situation and to develop successful strategies to achieve your goals.

Personal Action Plan

Date

Action Step 1

Develop your change scenario: A change scenario is a short essay about yourself similar to the comments you have read earlier. Write about what's happening in your life that is creating an interest in or a need to change. In other words, describe your opportunities for change.

....
....
....
....
....
....
....
....
....
....
....

Action Step 2

Describe your vision for change—your preferred future: What will happen to you as a result of the change you envision? When you write, imagine that the change has already taken place and describe what you or your situation look like as though it had already happened. Write, therefore, in the present tense. Describe how things look, how they differ from the way they used to be. And don't forget to indicate what month and year this is so that you will know how long you have given yourself to implement your vision for change.

....
....
....
....
....
....
....
....
....
....
....

Action Step 3   ***Translate your vision into goal statements:*** List your goals in the accompanying table and indicate whether they are for the short term (one to two years), the intermediate term (three to four years), or the long term (five or more years). Then restate those goals to indicate what they will look like when you've achieved them.

Goal number	Goal statement	How it will look when achieved	Time frame (years)		
			1–2	3–4	5+

Action Step 4   ***List in the accompanying table all positive or facilitating forces you can think of that will help you achieve each goal you have listed:*** Forces can be *within yourself* (I want to earn more money; I want to be promoted) or *within your family* (my children are grown up and out of the house; we need extra income to pay for our children's college) or *within your work or learning environment* (I have a new boss who demands that I get a college degree; I want to be able to compete with new employees who are better educated than I am). As you develop this analysis you will find that some forces are moving you toward more than one goal. It's not necessary to list a force more than once; just note all the goals each force facilitates.

Action Step 5   ***List in the accompanying table all negative or blocking forces that will impede your progress toward each goal you have identified:*** Again, it's not necessary to repeat any force that is blocking your progress toward more than one goal; just note all the goals each force is blocking. Some blocking forces we've heard about: "I'm frightened about the change." "I didn't go to school originally because I wasn't sure I would be successful." "My husband and children say they need me at home full-time." "My boss expects me to go to school, but my co-workers expect me to produce just as much and participate in extra overload assignments."

List all positive or facilitating forces	List all negative or blocking forces
Inside yourself	
Within your family and other relationships	
Within your work or learning environment	

Action Step 6 **Review Action Steps 4 and 5 and mark with an asterisk(*) the facilitating and blocking forces you can do something about immediately:** Focus on these forces first. As time goes on you can work on the others, but it's important to have a starting point. It's best to start with what can be changed *now*.

Action Step 7 **Mobilize for change:** Review the forces you marked with an asterisk (*) in Action Steps 4 and 5. Transfer the facilitating forces to the lefthand column of the following table. For each force you have recorded in the lefthand column, list all the ideas, means, and resources you can use to make these forces work more strongly for you.

Action Step 8 **Mobilize for change:** Review the forces you marked with an asterisk (*) in Action Steps 4 and 5. Transfer the blocking forces to the righthand column of the following table. For each force you have recorded in the righthand column, list all the ideas, means, and resources you can use to remove or cope with these forces.

Action Step 7   *Action Step 8*

Facilitating forces	Blocking forces
Force:	Force:
Force:	Force:
Force:	Force:

Action Step 9   ***Determine major change tactics:*** Review all of the information in Action Steps 7 and 8 and decide which ones are critical for achieving your goals. Write each of your change tactics in the accompanying table.

Action Step 10   ***Create a comprehensive action plan:*** Number the square in front of each change tactic to indicate the order in which these steps should be taken. After you have completed Action Steps 9 and 10, we suggest you rewrite your action plan in priority order, following the format of the accompanying table.

	Change tactics	Members of my change team who should be involved	Other resources available	Anticipated completion date
☐				
☐				
☐				
☐				
☐				
☐				
☐				
☐				
☐				
☐				
☐				

Action Step 11   ***Describe what early progress will look like for each change tactic:*** State each step in clear and concise terms that are oriented toward your end results.

Action Step 12   ***Keep things moving forward:*** Identify what needs to be done to keep things progressing toward your goals.

	Action Step 11	*Action Step 12*

Change tactic number	Progress description	What needs to be done to move ahead

Action Step 13   ***Review and revise your plan each week or as appropriate:*** This is a crucial step. As you proceed through school and face the challenges that lie ahead in your life, circumstances will change. There will be new goals and new forces that will help and hinder you, but you will be equipped with a powerful way to analyze the situation and to develop successful strategies to achieve your goals.

APPENDIX 2

Time-Management Forms

The filled-in material included in this appendix will serve as a guide as you complete your time-management forms.

The forms work together to provide an integrated, comprehensive system for effective time management. Two sets of blank forms are provided for your use.

Sharon's Plan

Term Planner

MONTH: December   YEAR: 19XX

	Sunday	Monday	Tuesday	Wednesday	Thursday	Friday	Saturday
				1	2	3	4
A.M.				(Paper due) 10 History 11 English	(NCG Word-processing project due)	10 History 11 English	✕
NOON							
P.M.				2 Pol Sci 3 Adult Learner Support group		2 Pol Sci	Ron's basketball playoff
EVE							

	Sunday	Monday	Tuesday	Wednesday	Thursday	Friday	Saturday
	5	6	7	8	9	10	11
A.M.	10 History 11 English		Jill dentist	10 History 11 English		10 History 11 English (Paper due)	✕
NOON				(BRI Word-processing project preliminary copy due)	(Class Group presentation)		
P.M.	2 Pol Sci			2 Pol Sci 3 Adult Learner Support group	2 Pol Sci	2 Pol Sci	
EVE							

	12	13	14	15	16	17	18
A.M.		10 History / 11 English	FINAL EXAMS BEGIN			10 (HISTORY FINAL)	✕
NOON							
P.M.		2 Pol Sci / (BRI Final copy due)				2 (POL SCI FINAL)	
EVE	Xmas shopping						

	19	20	21	22	23	24	25
A.M.		11 (ENGLISH FINAL)	HOORAY! Fall Term OVER!		Xmas shopping		Family Xmas dinner
NOON							
P.M.	Xmas shopping		Family celebration going to dinner!		House cleaning & decorating		
EVE							

	26	27	28	29	30	31	
A.M.						New Years Eve Party	
NOON							
P.M.							
EVE							

Time Planner

		a: How I plan my time			b: How I used my time		

	Monday		Tuesday		Wednesday		Thursday		Friday		Saturday		Sunday	
	a	b	a	b	a	b	a	b	a	b	a	b	a	b
A.M./6:00														
7:00	Get kids up and ready for school										P	W	O	W
8:00	S	S	W→	P	S	S	W	W	S	S	→	→O	→O	O
9:00	S	S			S	S	O	O	S	S	O	O	O	O
10:00	C	C	→O→		C	C	→	→	C	C	O	O	→O	O
11:00	C	C			C	C	O	O	C	C	O	O	→	
NOON/12:00	O→	O	O→	→	O→	S	O	O	O	O	→	O	→	
1:00	S	S			C→	O	→O	C	O→	C	O	O		
2:00	C	C			C	C	C	C	C	C				
3:00	P	S	W→	W	P	P	P	P	O	O				
4:00							—	—						
5:00	— Dinner and time with family —													
P.M./6:00	—													
7:00	S	S	S	W	W	W	S	S	O	O	O	O	O	O
8:00	O→	S	S→	W	W→	W	S→	S	O→	O	O→	O	S*→	S*→
9:00	S	S											S*	S*
10:00	→→												S*	S*
11:00														
A.M./12:00														

KEY: C, class; S, study; W, work; P, personal; O, other.

* Includes time for planning next week

Time Analysis

Item	a: How I planned my time		b: How I used my time	
	Number of hours	Percent*	Number of hours	Percent*
Class	9	5.4	9	5.4
Study	15	9.0	18	11.0
Work	16	9.5	27	16.0
Personal	9	5.4	4	2.4
Other	28	16.0	22	13.1
Total planned time	77/168		80/168	

*Base percent on the total of 168 hours in a week.

ANALYSIS: Describe what happened I stayed close to my plan & achieved my goals for the week — despite emergencies. I need to plan time to meet w/ student study groups, find out faculty office hours, & check out what is offered by Career Service center.

PLANS for reaching goals Check w/ classmates about times to study and schedule them into my plan. Find out faculty office hours so I can speak to my profs.

What I Need to Accomplish This Week: Dec. 5-11

Objectives	Time needed	Who and what I need to help me achieve objective	Notes
Academic: English paper due 10th	6.0	Need lots of free time	Review appual
Review all course notes for exams	3.0	If any info lacking - see other students to borrow & copy their notes	with prof
Read History material on reserve	2.0	Xerox material if more than 2 pages is needed	
Pol Sci presentation	1.30	Group meeting to review presentation	Arrange Mon.
Adult Learner Support Group	.30	Buy/bring goodies. Last meeting for Term	
Subtotal	13.0		
Personal: See if I can get someone to take Jill to dentist	.15	If no - schedule 2 hrs	
Aerobics at Rec/IM Center	2.0		Check to see if Sally going
Shop for X mas presents for Frida & Jim	4.0	$ $	
Subtotal	6.15		
Work: BRI - Prepare & submit preliminary copy.	6.0	Get Jim to obtain materials	
- Review & input edit changes	3.0	Get someone to watch kids Sat. afternoon	
Pick up materials (paper, etc.) for report	1.0	See if Jim will do this	
Subtotal	10.0		
Other: Plan for next week	.30	Need extra time OR convince everyone to wear dirty clothes!!	
Laundry & ironing	2.30		
Subtotal	3.0		
Total	32.15		

Daily Planner

DATE: Wed. 12-8

Schedule	Item no.
7	
30	O-1
8 Study	A-3
9 Study	A-1
10 History class	
11 English class	A-2
12 Finish Pol Sci project	A-1
1 Lunch	
2 Pol Sci class	
3 Adult Learner Support Group	P-1
4	
5 Dinner & time with family	
6	
7	
8 Work - Tell kids no interruptions tonight!	
9	

Academic assignments

A-1	Rehearse class group present.
A-2	See prof. re. Eng. paper
A-3	Read History summaries
A-4	
A-5	
A-6	
A-7	
A-8	
A-9	
A-10	
A-11	
A-12	
A-13	
A-14	

Personal items

P-1	Borrow X-mas gift catalogue (see if it is too late to order)
P-2	
P-3	
P-4	
P-5	
P-6	
P-7	
P-8	
P-9	
P-10	
P-11	
P-12	
P-13	
P-14	

Work items

W-1	Call to check on return
W-2	BRI project review will
W-3	be returned to me for
W-4	final prep.
W-5	
W-6	
W-7	
W-8	
W-9	
W-10	
W-11	
W-12	
W-13	
W-14	

Other

O-1	Prepare refreshments for Support Group
O-2	
O-3	
O-4	
O-5	
O-6	
O-7	
O-8	
O-9	
O-10	
O-11	
O-12	
O-13	
O-14	

Bruce's Plan

Term Planner

MONTH: October   YEAR: 19XX

	Sunday	Monday	Tuesday	Wednesday	Thursday	Friday	Saturday
A.M.						**1** 8AM Math / 9AM Speech / 11-6 Work ↓	**2**
NOON						Lunch	
P.M.							
EVE							
A.M.	**3** 8 Math / 9 Speech	**4** 8 Pol Sci	**5** 8 Math / 9 Speech	**6** 8 Pol Sci	**7** 8 Math / 9 Speech	**8**	**9**
NOON		11-6 Work + Lunch					
P.M.				(Pol Sci Paper Due)			Family Outing — Homecoming Football Game
EVE				7PM Lit			

A.M.	6 8 Math 9 Speech	7 8 Pol Sci	12 8 Math 9 Speech	13 8 Pol Sci	14 8 Math 9 Speech	15
NOON	11-6 Work Lunch				
P.M.					Persuasive Speech Due
EVE					16

A.M.	17 8 Math 9 Speech	18 8 Pol Sci 9 Speech	19 8 Math 9 Speech	20 8 Pol Sci 9 Speech	21 8 Math 9 Speech	22
NOON	11-6 Work + Lunch				
P.M.	Math Exam			Pol Sci Group Presentation	Family Outing – Zoo
EVE					23

A.M.	24/31 8 Math 9 Speech	25 8 Pol Sci	26 8 Math 9 Speech	27 8 Pol Sci	28 8 Math 9 Speech	29
NOON	1-6 Work + Lunch				
P.M.			Lit Mid Term		30
EVE			7pm Lit		

Time Planner

a: How I plan my time
b: How I used my time

Get ready for day — Take Jen to Day Care

Dinner time with family

	Monday		Tuesday		Wednesday		Thursday		Friday		Saturday		Sunday	
	a	b	a	b	a	b	a	b	a	b	a	b	a	b
A.M./6:00														
7:00	C	C	C	C	C	C	C	C	C	C	P	P	O	O
8:00		⊤	C	C	C	C	C	C	C	⊤	O	⊤	O	P
9:00	O	O		⊤	C	⊤	C	⊤	C	O				⊤
10:00	W	W	O	O	O	O	O	O	O	W	S	P	P	
11:00			W	W	W	W	W	W	W					⊤
NOON/12:00													S	
1:00											P	⊤		S
2:00														⊤
3:00														
4:00		⊤		⊤		⊤		⊤		⊤				
5:00														
P.M./6:00	P	P	P	P	C	C	P	P	P	P	P		S	O
7:00	S	S	S	S	C	C	S	S	P	P	P		S	S
8:00		⊤		⊤			P	P		⊤		⊤		⊤
9:00	S	S	S	S	S	S	S	S						
10:00				⊤		⊤				⊤				
11:00		⊤						⊤						
A.M./12:00														

KEY: C, class; S, study; W, work; P, personal; O, other.

Time Analysis

Item	a: How I planned my time		b: How I used my time	
	Number of hours	Percent*	Number of hours	Percent*
Class	13	8%	13	8%
Study	19	11%	19	11%
Work	35	21%	35	21%
Personal	23	14%	27	16%
Other	13	8%	11	7%
Total planned time	103	61%	105	63%

*Base percent on the total of 168 hours in a week.

ANALYSIS: Describe what happened   I stayed fairly close to my schedule but I realized that my schedule leaves little room for unplanned activities. Staying after class on Thurs. almost made me late for work. Taking 4 courses is tough; I feel really locked in!

PLANS for reaching goals   Need to plan time for next week with more flexibility — Wednesday was a killer day. See if I can get out of driving to day care on Wednesdays.

What I Need to Accomplish This Week: Oct. 11-23

Objectives	Time needed	Who and what I need to help me achieve objective	Notes
Academic:			
Study for math exam (18th)	4.0	Q niet time to review	Have all HW
Speech class preparation + reading	3.0	homework problems	problem ans. avail.
Prepare for Pol Sci group presentation (21st)	4.0	Meet w group after class on Tues; get overhead slides made.	
Read for Lit class	8.0		
Subtotal	19.0		
Personal:			
Bowling w team from work on Friday	3.0	Find babysitter	*Call Susie
Take family to the zoo on Sunday	5.0	Need good weather + picnic lunch!	
Subtotal	8.0		
Work:			
Clean up Oliver file	2.0	Talk to Jim in Purchasing	
Look into computer application problem	2.0	Call Betty in Info. Systems	
Subtotal	4.0		
Other:			
Develop plan for next week	1.0		
Subtotal	1.0		
Total	32.0		

Daily Planner

DATE: _Oct. 19_

	Schedule	Item no.
7	Take Jen to day care	
8	Pol. Sci. class	A-1
9	(9:15) Meet w̄ group for Pol. Sci.	A-2
10		
11	Work	W-4
12		
1		
2		
3		P-1
4		
5		
6	Dinner	
7	Study	A-3
8		A-4
9		

Academic assignments

A-1	Read ch 4 (Pol. Sci.)
A-2	Group presentation (Pol. Sci.)
A-3	Math: ch 6 prob 6, 8, 10, 12
A-4	Speech: read article
A-5	
A-6	
A-7	
A-8	
A-9	
A-10	
A-11	
A-12	
A-13	
A-14	

Personal items

P-1	Make arrangements to go to zoo on Sat.
P-2	
P-3	
P-4	
P-5	
P-6	
P-7	
P-8	
P-9	
P-10	
P-11	
P-12	
P-13	
P-14	

Work items

W-1	Mtg. w Oliver (3:00 P.M.) re: new orders
W-2	
W-3	
W-4	Prepare W-6 5 form for NW distribution
W-5	
W-6	
W-7	
W-8	
W-9	
W-10	
W-11	
W-12	
W-13	
W-14	

Other

O-1	
O-2	
O-3	
O-4	
O-5	
O-6	
O-7	
O-8	
O-9	
O-10	
O-11	
O-12	
O-13	
O-14	

Term Planner

MONTH: _____   YEAR: _____

	Sunday	Monday	Tuesday	Wednesday	Thursday	Friday	Saturday
A.M.							
NOON							
P.M.							
EVE							
A.M.							
NOON							
P.M.							
EVE							

A.M.

NOON

P.M.

EVE

A.M.

NOON

P.M.

EVE

A.M.

NOON

P.M.

EVE

Time Planner

a: How I plan my time

b: How I used my time

	Monday		Tuesday		Wednesday		Thursday		Friday		Saturday		Sunday	
	a	*b*	*a*	*b*	*a*	*b*	*a*	*b*	*a*	*b*	*a*	*b*	*a*	*b*
A.M./6:00														
7:00														
8:00														
9:00														
10:00														
11:00														
NOON/12:00														
1:00														
2:00														
3:00														
4:00														
5:00														
P.M./6:00														
7:00														
8:00														
9:00														
10:00														
11:00														
A.M./12:00														

KEY: C, class; S, study; W, work; P, personal; O, other.

Time Analysis

Item	a: How I planned my time		b: How I used my time	
	Number of hours	Percent*	Number of hours	Percent*
Class				
Study				
Work				
Personal				
Other				
Total planned time				

*Base percent on the total of 168 hours in a week.

ANALYSIS: Describe what happened

PLANS for reaching goals

What I Need to Accomplish This Week:

Objectives	Time needed	Who and what I need to help me achieve objective	Notes
Academic:			
Subtotal			
Personal:			
Subtotal			
Work:			
Subtotal			
Other:			
Subtotal			
Total			

Daily Planner

DATE: ....

Schedule	Item no.	Academic assignments		Work items	
7		A-1		W-1	
		A-2		W-2	
8		A-3		W-3	
		A-4		W-4	
9		A-5		W-5	
		A-6		W-6	
10		A-7		W-7	
		A-8		W-8	
11		A-9		W-9	
		A-10		W-10	
12		A-11		W-11	
		A-12		W-12	
1		A-13		W-13	
		A-14		W-14	
2		Personal items		Other	
3		P-1		O-1	
		P-2		O-2	
4		P-3		O-3	
		P-4		O-4	
5		P-5		O-5	
		P-6		O-6	
6		P-7		O-7	
		P-8		O-8	
7		P-9		O-9	
		P-10		O-10	
8		P-11		O-11	
		P-12		O-12	
9		P-13		O-13	
		P-14		O-14	

Daily Planner

DATE: _____

Schedule

Item no.		
7		
8		
9		
10		
11		
12		
1		
2		
3		
4		
5		
6		
7		
8		
9		

Academic assignments

A-1	
A-2	
A-3	
A-4	
A-5	
A-6	
A-7	
A-8	
A-9	
A-10	
A-11	
A-12	
A-13	
A-14	

Personal items

P-1	
P-2	
P-3	
P-4	
P-5	
P-6	
P-7	
P-8	
P-9	
P-10	
P-11	
P-12	
P-13	
P-14	

Work items

W-1	
W-2	
W-3	
W-4	
W-5	
W-6	
W-7	
W-8	
W-9	
W-10	
W-11	
W-12	
W-13	
W-14	

Other

O-1	
O-2	
O-3	
O-4	
O-5	
O-6	
O-7	
O-8	
O-9	
O-10	
O-11	
O-12	
O-13	
O-14	

Daily Planner

DATE:

Schedule	Item no.	Academic assignments	Work items
7		A-1	W-1
		A-2	W-2
8		A-3	W-3
		A-4	W-4
9		A-5	W-5
		A-6	W-6
10		A-7	W-7
		A-8	W-8
11		A-9	W-9
		A-10	W-10
12		A-11	W-11
		A-12	W-12
1		A-13	W-13
		A-14	W-14
2			
		Personal items	Other
3		P-1	O-1
		P-2	O-2
4		P-3	O-3
		P-4	O-4
5		P-5	O-5
		P-6	O-6
6		P-7	O-7
		P-8	O-8
7		P-9	O-9
		P-10	O-10
8		P-11	O-11
		P-12	O-12
9		P-13	O-13
		P-14	O-14

Daily Planner

DATE: ....

Schedule	Item no.	Academic assignments	Work items
7		A-1	W-1
		A-2	W-2
8		A-3	W-3
		A-4	W-4
9		A-5	W-5
		A-6	W-6
10		A-7	W-7
		A-8	W-8
11		A-9	W-9
		A-10	W-10
12		A-11	W-11
		A-12	W-12
1		A-13	W-13
		A-14	W-14
2		Personal items	Other
3		P-1	O-1
		P-2	O-2
4		P-3	O-3
		P-4	O-4
5		P-5	O-5
		P-6	O-6
6		P-7	O-7
		P-8	O-8
7		P-9	O-9
		P-10	O-10
8		P-11	O-11
		P-12	O-12
9		P-13	O-13
		P-14	O-14

Daily Planner

DATE: ....

Schedule	Item no.
7	
8	
9	
10	
11	
12	
1	
2	
3	
4	
5	
6	
7	
8	
9	

Academic assignments

A-1
A-2
A-3
A-4
A-5
A-6
A-7
A-8
A-9
A-10
A-11
A-12
A-13
A-14

Work items

W-1
W-2
W-3
W-4
W-5
W-6
W-7
W-8
W-9
W-10
W-11
W-12
W-13
W-14

Personal items

P-1
P-2
P-3
P-4
P-5
P-6
P-7
P-8
P-9
P-10
P-11
P-12
P-13
P-14

Other

O-1
O-2
O-3
O-4
O-5
O-6
O-7
O-8
O-9
O-10
O-11
O-12
O-13
O-14

Daily Planner

DATE: _____

Schedule	Item no.
7	
8	
9	
10	
11	
12	
1	
2	
3	
4	
5	
6	
7	
8	
9	

Academic assignments	Work items
A-1	W-1
A-2	W-2
A-3	W-3
A-4	W-4
A-5	W-5
A-6	W-6
A-7	W-7
A-8	W-8
A-9	W-9
A-10	W-10
A-11	W-11
A-12	W-12
A-13	W-13
A-14	W-14

Personal items	Other
P-1	O-1
P-2	O-2
P-3	O-3
P-4	O-4
P-5	O-5
P-6	O-6
P-7	O-7
P-8	O-8
P-9	O-9
P-10	O-10
P-11	O-11
P-12	O-12
P-13	O-13
P-14	O-14

Daily Planner

DATE:

Schedule	Item no.
7	
8	
9	
10	
11	
12	
1	
2	
3	
4	
5	
6	
7	
8	
9	

Academic assignments

A-1
A-2
A-3
A-4
A-5
A-6
A-7
A-8
A-9
A-10
A-11
A-12
A-13
A-14

Personal items

P-1
P-2
P-3
P-4
P-5
P-6
P-7
P-8
P-9
P-10
P-11
P-12
P-13
P-14

Work items

W-1
W-2
W-3
W-4
W-5
W-6
W-7
W-8
W-9
W-10
W-11
W-12
W-13
W-14

Other

O-1
O-2
O-3
O-4
O-5
O-6
O-7
O-8
O-9
O-10
O-11
O-12
O-13
O-14

Term Planner

MONTH: _____   YEAR: _____

	Sunday	Monday	Tuesday	Wednesday	Thursday	Friday	Saturday
A.M.							
NOON							
P.M.							
EVE							
A.M.							
NOON							
P.M.							
EVE							

A.M.

NOON

P.M.

EVE

A.M.

NOON

P.M.

EVE

A.M.

NOON

P.M.

EVE

Time Planner

a: How I plan my time   *b:* How I used my time

	Monday		Tuesday		Wednesday		Thursday		Friday		Saturday		Sunday	
	a	*b*	*a*	*b*	*a*	*b*	*a*	*b*	*a*	*b*	*a*	*b*	*a*	*b*
A.M./6:00														
7:00														
8:00														
9:00														
10:00														
11:00														
NOON/12:00														
1:00														
2:00														
3:00														
4:00														
5:00														
P.M./6:00														
7:00														
8:00														
9:00														
10:00														
11:00														
A.M./12:00														

KEY: C, class; S, study; W, work; P, personal; O, other.

Time Analysis

Item	a: How I planned my time		b: How I used my time	
	Number of hours	Percent*	Number of hours	Percent*
Class				
Study				
Work				
Personal				
Other				
Total planned time				

*Base percent on the total of 168 hours in a week.

ANALYSIS: Describe what happened

PLANS for reaching goals

What I Need to Accomplish This Week: _____

Objectives	Time needed	Who and what I need to help me achieve objective	Notes
Academic:			
Subtotal			
Personal:			
Subtotal			
Work:			
Subtotal			
Other:			
Subtotal			
Total			

Daily Planner

DATE: ....

Schedule		Item no.
7		
8		
9		
10		
11		
12		
1		
2		
3		
4		
5		
6		
7		
8		
9		

Academic assignments

A-1	
A-2	
A-3	
A-4	
A-5	
A-6	
A-7	
A-8	
A-9	
A-10	
A-11	
A-12	
A-13	
A-14	

Work items

W-1	
W-2	
W-3	
W-4	
W-5	
W-6	
W-7	
W-8	
W-9	
W-10	
W-11	
W-12	
W-13	
W-14	

Personal items

P-1	
P-2	
P-3	
P-4	
P-5	
P-6	
P-7	
P-8	
P-9	
P-10	
P-11	
P-12	
P-13	
P-14	

Other

O-1	
O-2	
O-3	
O-4	
O-5	
O-6	
O-7	
O-8	
O-9	
O-10	
O-11	
O-12	
O-13	
O-14	

Daily Planner

DATE: _____

Schedule	Item no.	Academic assignments		Work items
7		A-1		W-1
8		A-2		W-2
9		A-3		W-3
10		A-4		W-4
11		A-5		W-5
12		A-6		W-6
1		A-7		W-7
2		A-8		W-8
3		A-9		W-9
4		A-10		W-10
5		A-11		W-11
6		A-12		W-12
7		A-13		W-13
8		A-14		W-14
9				

Personal items	Other
P-1	O-1
P-2	O-2
P-3	O-3
P-4	O-4
P-5	O-5
P-6	O-6
P-7	O-7
P-8	O-8
P-9	O-9
P-10	O-10
P-11	O-11
P-12	O-12
P-13	O-13
P-14	O-14

Daily Planner

DATE: _____

Schedule	Item no.	Academic assignments		Work items	
7		A-1		W-1	
		A-2		W-2	
8		A-3		W-3	
		A-4		W-4	
9		A-5		W-5	
		A-6		W-6	
10		A-7		W-7	
		A-8		W-8	
11		A-9		W-9	
		A-10		W-10	
12		A-11		W-11	
		A-12		W-12	
1		A-13		W-13	
		A-14		W-14	
2		Personal items		Other	
3		P-1		O-1	
		P-2		O-2	
4		P-3		O-3	
		P-4		O-4	
5		P-5		O-5	
		P-6		O-6	
6		P-7		O-7	
		P-8		O-8	
7		P-9		O-9	
		P-10		O-10	
8		P-11		O-11	
		P-12		O-12	
9		P-13		O-13	
		P-14		O-14	

Daily Planner

DATE: ....

Schedule	Item no.	Academic assignments		Work items	
7		A-1		W-1	
		A-2		W-2	
8		A-3		W-3	
		A-4		W-4	
9		A-5		W-5	
		A-6		W-6	
10		A-7		W-7	
		A-8		W-8	
11		A-9		W-9	
		A-10		W-10	
12		A-11		W-11	
		A-12		W-12	
1		A-13		W-13	
		A-14		W-14	
2					
		Personal items		Other	
3		P-1		O-1	
		P-2		O-2	
4		P-3		O-3	
		P-4		O-4	
5		P-5		O-5	
		P-6		O-6	
6		P-7		O-7	
		P-8		O-8	
7		P-9		O-9	
		P-10		O-10	
8		P-11		O-11	
		P-12		O-12	
9		P-13		O-13	
		P-14		O-14	

Daily Planner

DATE: _____

Schedule		Item no.
7		
8		
9		
10		
11		
12		
1		
2		
3		
4		
5		
6		
7		
8		
9		

Academic assignments

A-1	
A-2	
A-3	
A-4	
A-5	
A-6	
A-7	
A-8	
A-9	
A-10	
A-11	
A-12	
A-13	
A-14	

Work items

W-1	
W-2	
W-3	
W-4	
W-5	
W-6	
W-7	
W-8	
W-9	
W-10	
W-11	
W-12	
W-13	
W-14	

Personal items

P-1	
P-2	
P-3	
P-4	
P-5	
P-6	
P-7	
P-8	
P-9	
P-10	
P-11	
P-12	
P-13	
P-14	

Other

O-1	
O-2	
O-3	
O-4	
O-5	
O-6	
O-7	
O-8	
O-9	
O-10	
O-11	
O-12	
O-13	
O-14	

Daily Planner

DATE: ....

Item no.	Schedule	Academic assignments		Work items
7		A-1		W-1
8		A-2		W-2
9		A-3		W-3
10		A-4		W-4
11		A-5		W-5
12		A-6		W-6
1		A-7		W-7
2		A-8		W-8
3		A-9		W-9
4		A-10		W-10
5		A-11		W-11
6		A-12		W-12
7		A-13		W-13
8		A-14		W-14
9				

Personal items		Other
P-1		O-1
P-2		O-2
P-3		O-3
P-4		O-4
P-5		O-5
P-6		O-6
P-7		O-7
P-8		O-8
P-9		O-9
P-10		O-10
P-11		O-11
P-12		O-12
P-13		O-13
P-14		O-14

Daily Planner

DATE: ....

Schedule	Item no.
7	
8	
9	
10	
11	
12	
1	
2	
3	
4	
5	
6	
7	
8	
9	

Academic assignments

A-1
A-2
A-3
A-4
A-5
A-6
A-7
A-8
A-9
A-10
A-11
A-12
A-13
A-14

Personal items

P-1
P-2
P-3
P-4
P-5
P-6
P-7
P-8
P-9
P-10
P-11
P-12
P-13
P-14

Work items

W-1
W-2
W-3
W-4
W-5
W-6
W-7
W-8
W-9
W-10
W-11
W-12
W-13
W-14

Other

O-1
O-2
O-3
O-4
O-5
O-6
O-7
O-8
O-9
O-10
O-11
O-12
O-13
O-14

APPENDIX 3

Reading Excerpt from Introduction to Psychology *by James Kalat*

To be used with Chapter 11, Strategy 5 (p. 89)

How Thought Processes and Knowledge Grow: Some Piagetian Terminology

According to Piaget, a child's intellectual development is not merely an accumulation of experience or a maturational unfolding. Rather, the child constructs *new* mental processes as he or she interacts with the environment.

In Piaget's terminology, behavior is based on schemata. A **schema** is an organized way of interacting with objects in the world. For instance, infants have a grasping schema and a sucking schema. Older infants gradually add new schemata to their repertoire and adapt their old ones. This adaptation takes place through the processes of assimilation and accommodation.

In **assimilation** a person applies an old schema to new objects—for example, an infant may suck an unfamiliar object or use the grasp response in trying to manipulate it. In **accommodation** a person modifies an old schema to fit a new object—for example, an infant may suck a breast, a bottle, and a pacifier in different ways or may modify the grasp response to accommodate the size or shape of a new toy.

Infants shift back and forth from assimilation to accommodation. For example, an infant who tries to suck on a rubber ball (assimilating it to her sucking schema) may find that she cannot fit it into her mouth. First she may try to accommodate her sucking schema to fit the ball; if that fails, she may try to shake the ball. She is assimilating her grasping schema to the new object—expanding her motor repertoire to include it—but at the same time she is accommodating that schema—changing it—to fit the ball.

Adults do much the same thing. You are given a new mathematical problem to solve. You try several of the methods you have already learned until you hit on the one schema that works. In other words, you assimilate your old schema to the new problem. If, however, the new problem is quite different from any problem you have ever solved before, you modify (accommodate) your schema until you work out a solution. Through processes like these, said Piaget, intellectual growth occurs.

Piaget's Stages of Intellectual Development

Piaget contended that children progress through four major stages of intellectual development:

1. The sensorimotor stage (from birth to about 1½ years)
2. The preoperational stage (from about 1½ to 7 years)
3. The concrete operations stage (from about 7 to 11 years)
4. The formal operations stage (from about 11 years onward)

The ages given here are approximate. Many people do not reach the stage of formal operations until well beyond age 11, if they reach it at all. Piaget recognized that some children develop at a faster rate than others, but he insisted that all children go through these four stages *in the same order*. Exactly how distinct the stages are is not clear (Keil, 1981).

The Sensorimotor Stage: Infancy Piaget called the first stage of intellectual development the **sensorimotor stage** because at this early age (birth to 1½ years) behavior consists mostly of simple motor responses to sensory stimuli—for example, the grasp reflex and the sucking reflex. Infants respond to what is present, rather than to what is remembered or imagined. Piaget concluded that infants in the sensorimotor stage are incapable of representational thought—that is, they do not think about objects they cannot see, hear, feel, or otherwise sense. Moreover, Piaget concluded that infants lack the concept of **object permanence.** They do not understand that an object continues to exist when they can no longer see it. (Not only is it "out of sight, out of mind," but "out of sight, out of existence" as well.)

How, you might ask, can we possibly know what a baby does or does not think? We cannot—at least, not for sure. Piaget was drawing inferences from the behavior he observed, though other people have drawn different inferences. After we review Piaget's observations, you can draw your own conclusions. (Better yet, study a baby to make your own observations.)

1. *Observation:* From age 3 months to age 6 to 9 months, an infant will reach out to grab a toy only if it is visible. If the toy is partially visible, the infant will reach for it; if it is fully hidden, however, the infant will not reach for it even after watching someone hide it (Piaget, 1937/1954). *Piaget's interpretation:* An infant who does not see an object does not know it is there. *Other possible interpretations:* The infant may know the object still exists but may not remember *where* it is. Or the infant may be distracted by other objects that *are* visible.

2. *Observation:* If we hide a toy under a clear glass, most infants will lift the glass to get the toy; if we hide it under an opaque glass, most infants will make no effort to get it. *Possible interpretation:* Infants do not ignore a covered toy because they are unable to remove the cover. They ignore it because they do not see it.

3. *Observation:* If we show an infant a toy and then turn off the lights before the infant can grab it, the infant will still reach out to grab it in the dark (Bower & Wishart, 1972). *Possible interpretation:* Contrary to the first two observations, this one seems to indicate that infants will reach for something they remember but cannot see, provided they can see nothing else. In the first two cases, objects that remain visible may distract the infant from objects that are no longer visible.

4. *Observation:* From about 9 to 11 months, an infant who watches you hide a toy will reach out to retrieve it. But if you hide the toy first on the right side and then on the left side, the infant will reach out both times to the right side. *One interpretation:* Even at this age, infants do not fully understand that an object remains where it was hidden. *Another interpretation:* Infants know the object has been hidden but cannot remember where.

The Preoperational Stage: Early Childhood

Around age 1½ years, children reach a landmark in their intellectual development: They begin to acquire language at a rapid rate. Susan Carey (1978) has estimated that children between the ages of 1½ and 6 learn an average of nine new words *per day*—almost one new word per hour—thereby increasing their ability to tell us what they know and think (see Table 1). The fact that they can now talk about the properties of unseen objects is evidence that they have acquired the concept of object permanence. But there remain many things they do not understand at this age. For example, they have difficulty understanding that a mother can be someone else's daughter. A boy with one brother will assert that his brother has no brother. A child may say that there are more girls in a class than there are children. Piaget refers to this period as the **preoperational stage.** The child is said to lack **operations,** which are reversible mental processes. For example, for a boy to understand that his brother has a brother, he must be able to reverse the concept "having a brother."

Table 1 Conversations with Some Children at the Preoperational Stage

Q. Are you an American?
A. No, my father is an American. I'm a girl.

Q. Do you have to go to the bathroom?
A. Do. Don't have to go. Mine peanut not working. Don't have any juice in it.

Q. Do you understand what's happening in this movie (a nature film)?
A. Yes. When the baby skunks grow up, they turn into raccoons.

Children at this age generally accept their experiences at face value. A child who sees you put a white ball behind a blue filter will say that the ball is blue. When you ask, "Yes, I know the ball looks blue, but what color is it *really?*" the child grows confused. So far as the child is concerned, any ball that *looks* blue *is* blue (Flavell, 1986).

According to Piaget, preoperational children lack the concept of **conservation.** Just as they fail to understand that something can still be white even though it looks blue, they fail to understand that objects conserve such properties as number, length, volume, area, and mass after the shape or arrangement of the objects has changed. They cannot perform the mental operations necessary to understand such transformations. (Table 2 shows some typical conservation tasks.)

For example, if we arrange two equal rows of pennies and ask which row contains more pennies, nearly all preoperational children will answer that the rows contain the same number of pennies. But if we spread one row out, they answer confidently that the longer row has more pennies. They do not even see a need to count the pennies to check their answer. Once we ask them to count the pennies, they discover that the number has remained the same (Gelman & Baillargeon, 1983). (Parents sometimes make use of a child's lack of conservation. A preoperational child has a cookie and asks for another one. The parent breaks the cookie in half and says, "Here. Now you have two cookies." At least some children seem satisfied.)

If we set up two glasses of the same size containing the same amount of water and then pour the contents of one glass into a different-shaped glass, preoperational children will say that the taller, thinner glass contains more water.

I once doubted whether children really believed what they were saying in such a situation. Perhaps, I thought, the way the questions are phrased somehow tricks them into saying something they do not believe. Then something happened to convince me that preoperational children really believe their answers. One year, when I was discussing Piaget in my introductory psychology class, I invited my son Sam, then 5½ years old, to take part in a class demonstration. I started with two glasses of water, which he agreed contained equal amounts of water. Then I poured the water from one glass into a wider glass, lowering the water level. When I asked Sam which glass contained more water, he confidently pointed to the tall, thin one. After class he complained, "Daddy, why did you ask me such an easy question? Everyone could see that there was more water in that glass! You should have asked me something harder to show how smart I am!"

The following year I brought Sam to class again for the same demonstration. He was now 6½ years old, about the age at which children make the transition from preoperational thinking to the next stage. I again poured the water from one of the tall glasses into a wider one and asked him which glass contained more water. He looked and paused. His face got red. Finally he whispered, "Daddy, I don't know!"

Table 2 Typical Tasks Used to Measure Conservation

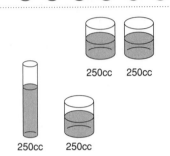

Conservation of number

Preoperational children say that the two rows have the same number of pennies.

Preoperational children say that the second row has more pennies.

Conservation of volume

Preoperational children say that the two same-size containers have the same amount of water.

Preoperational children say that the taller, thinner container has more water.

250cc   250cc

250cc   250cc

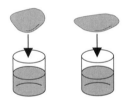

Conservation of mass

Preoperational children say that the two same-size balls of clay have the same amount of clay.

Preoperational children say that a squashed ball of clay contains a different amount of clay from the same-size round ball of clay.

Conservation of mass—water displacement

A child in the early part of the concrete-operations stage may know that a round ball of clay and one that has been squashed contain the same amount of clay.

However, the same child may think that the round and the squashed balls of clay will displace different amounts of water.

After class he complained, "Why did you ask me such a hard question? I'm never coming back to any of your classes again!" The question that was embarrassingly easy a year ago had become embarrassingly difficult.

The next year, when he was 7½, I tried again. This time he answered confidently, "Both glasses have the same amount of water, of course. Why? Is this some sort of trick question?"

The Concrete-Operations Stage: Later Childhood

At about age 7, children enter the stage of concrete operations and begin to understand the conservation of physical properties. The transition is not sharp, however. The ability to understand the conservation of various properties emerges sequentially, at different ages. For instance, a 6-year-old child may understand that squashing a ball of clay will not change its weight but may not realize until years later that squashing the ball will not change the volume of water it displaces when it is dropped into a glass.

The **stage of concrete operations** is Piaget's term for the stage when children can perform mental operations on concrete objects. But they still have trouble with abstract or hypothetical ideas. For example, ask a child at this stage, "If you had five six-headed dogs, how many heads would there be?" Even a child who has no difficulty multiplying 5 times 6 is likely to object. "But there is no such thing as a six-headed dog!"

Or ask this question: "How could you move a 4-mile-high mound of whipped cream from one side of the city to the other?" Older children find the question amusing and try to think of an imaginative answer. But children in the concrete-operations stage (or younger) are likely to complain that the question is silly or stupid.

Table 3 Summary of Piaget's Stages of Cognitive Development

Stage and approximate age	Achievements and activities	Limitations
Sensorimotor (birth to 1½ years)	Reacts to sensory stimuli through reflexes and other responses	Little use of language; seems not to understand object permanence; does not distinguish appearance from reality
Preoperational (1½ to 7 years)	Develops language; can represent objects mentally by words and other symbols; can respond to objects that are remembered but not present at the moment	Lacks operations (reversible mental processes); lacks concept of conservation; focuses on one property at a time (such as length or width), not on both at once; still has some trouble distinguishing appearance from reality
Concrete operations (7 to 11 years)	Understands conservation of mass, number, and volume; can reason logically with regard to concrete objects that can be seen or touched	Has trouble reasoning about abstract concepts and hypothetical situations
Formal operations (11 years onward)	Can reason logically about abstract and hypothetical concepts; develops strategies; plans actions in advance	None beyond the occasional irrationalities of all human thought

Or ask, "If you could have a third eye anywhere on your body, where would you put it?" Children in this stage generally respond immediately that they would put it right between the other two, on their forehead. They seem to regard the question as not very interesting. Older children come up with more imaginative possibilities, such as on the back of their head or at the top of a finger (so they could peek around corners).

The Formal-Operations Stage: Adolescence and Adulthood The **stage of formal operations** is Piaget's term referring to the mental processes used in dealing with abstract, hypothetical situations. Those processes demand logical, deductive reasoning and systematic planning.

Piaget set the beginning of the formal-operations stage at about age 11. He attributed some fairly sophisticated abilities to children in this stage, although later research indicates that many children take much longer to reach it and some people never do get there.

Suppose we ask three children, ages 6, 10, and 14, to arrange a set of 12 sticks in order from longest to shortest. The 6-year-old (preoperational) child fails to order the sticks correctly. The 10-year-old (concrete operations) eventually gets them in the right order, but only after a great deal of trial and error. The 14-year-old (formal operations) holds the sticks upright with their bottom ends on the table and then removes the longest one, the second-longest one, and so on.

A second example: We set up five bottles of clear liquid and explain that it is possible, by mixing the liquids together in a certain combination, to produce a yellow liquid. The task is to find the right combination. Children in the concrete-operations stage plunge right in with an unsystematic trial-and-error search. They try combining bottles A and B, then C and D, then perhaps A, C, and E, and so on. By the time they work through five or six combinations they forget which ones they have already tried. They may try one combination several times and others not at all; if and when they do stumble onto the correct combination, it is mostly a matter of luck.

Children in the formal-operations stage approach the problem more systematically. They may first try all the two-bottle combinations: AB, AC, AD, AE, BC, and so forth. If all those fail, they turn to three-bottle combinations: ABC, ABD, ABE, ACD, and so on. By adopting a strategy for trying every possible combination one time and one time only, they are bound to succeed.

Children do not reach the stage of formal operations any more suddenly than they reach the concrete-operations stage. Before they can reason logically about a particular problem, they must first have had a fair amount of experience in dealing with that problem. A 9-year-old who has spent a great deal of time playing chess reasons logically about chess problems and plans several moves ahead. The same child reverts to concrete reasoning when faced with an unfamiliar problem.

Table 3 summarizes Piaget's four stages.

SOURCE: From *Introduction to Psychology,* Second Edition by James W. Kalat. Copyright © 1990, 1986 by Wadsworth, Inc. Pages 196–200 reprinted by permission of the publisher.